YOU'RE
IN
AMERICA

NOW WHAT?

YOU'RE IN AMERICA

NOW WHAT?

7 Skills to Integrate with EASE & JOY

SENAIT MESFIN PICCIGALLO

FOREWORD BY
Yonas B. Keleta, PhD
Associate professor of Behavioral Neuroscience
Research and Datamining Consultant

KP PUBLISHING COMPANY

Disclaimers:
This book is a work of nonfiction. Real names have been used with permission and in some instances fictitious names have been used for privacy purposes.

The words, "The Immigrant" the author is referring to people who came to the USA as refugees, asylees, or any other status to eventually live as Americans.

The author is not a mental health professional. She is sharing her mental health experience and it should not be used as a replacement for care from a mental health care professional.

ISBN: 978-1-950936-46-5
Library of Congress Control Number:

Editor: KP Publishing Services
Cover Design: Juan Roberts, Creative Lunacy
Literary Director: Sandra Slayton James
Interior Design: Jennifer Houle
Photography: Tymn Urban Design

Published by:
KP Publishing Company
Publisher of Fiction, Nonfiction & Children's Books
Valencia, CA 91355
www.kp-pub.com

Printed in the United States of America

This book is dedicated to the memory of
Saliem Tesfay Ghebreigzher

CONTENTS

Contents

YOU'RE IN AMERICA — *NOW WHAT?*

FOREWORD

It's been a little over twenty-three years since the author of this book, Senait Mesfin Piccigallo, and I met for the first time inside the Main Campus of Asmara University. It was mid of 1998, one of the most challenging times for the people of Eritrea and Ethiopia. This time, Senait and I, along with several friends and roommates, served the UNHCR (United Nations High Commissioner for Refugees) as volunteers helping Eritrean deportees from Ethiopia. Almost all the volunteers were born and raised in Ethiopia, and communicating with the deportees from Ethiopia and taking information relevant to the refugee's organization was not a problem. Furthermore, we all had good relationships and camaraderie because we grew up in the same culture and spoke the same language. That is why Senait and I clicked at the first instance.

After I graduated with a bachelor's degree in Animal Sciences, I left Eritrea in January 2001, when the war between the two nations ended but with a state of "No War No Peace." Like any other immigrant, I have faced almost all the challenges covered in this book in-depth. But I also was lucky enough to get some help and support from some American friends and some Eritreans as well—I highly appreciate the financial and moral support I received from these people. I had no housing and financial issues for the first three months. After three months, however, I got two part-time jobs in Boston; one at Au Bon Pain as a shift supervisor, and another at Garage at Post Office Square as a night-shift manager. After working two jobs and attending the University of Massachusetts (UMASS) Boston, I decided to move to San Antonio, Texas, for full-time schooling at the University of Texas at San Antonio (UTSA). Because I was so dedicated to earning the highest level of education, I finally managed to receive my doctorate (PhD) in Neurobiology, with an emphasis on Dopamine Neurons and neural circuits of reinforcement learning and drug addiction. Long story short, I moved from Texas to California (Bay Area) due to a job opportunity. I am now serving as an associate professor in the field of Neuroscience. My teaching expertise now extends overseas, as well. I serve as an associate professor of Neurobiology and Biochemistry at ZheJiang Normal University in China.

Senait and I met up again in San Jose, California, after almost eight years. It was a blessing to find an old friend after such a long time! I had the privilege of being the honored guest to speak on Cerebral Palsy at Aaron's Foundation Inauguration in 2014.

When I read Senait's book entitled ***You're in America - Now What? 7 Skills to Integrate with Ease & Joy*** my first impression was that I wish I had this kind of resource before moving to the US to make my cultural integration a lot smoother. I have never seen or read a book that is so well written and well thought out to make the life of an immigrant simpler! I highly recommend immigrants from all corners of the world to use it as a reference to make the process of their cultural integration a lot easier and joyful! The author walks you through many essential topics that the immigrant needs to know to make their life journey more successful. To make your cultural integration process easier in a foreign society, Senait gives us some "YOU NEED TO KNOW" basic tips. Included are several topics on maintaining a positive attitude, managing and controlling one's emotions, how and where to obtain your support system, and eventually building self-confidence, allowing one to integrate within a sea of diverse communities easily and freely where they live.

What I like most about Senait is that despite all the odds she managed to handle along her life journey, she showed the audacity to share the ups and downs of her path vividly, so other newcomers learn from her experience. Senait shares her struggles while raising her son with Cerebral Palsy, how far she traveled to get his medication, how she dealt with mental health-related issues and cultural shocks in the process of integration in a foreign environment, and more. All of the above clearly shows the manifestations of her strength, open-mindedness to inexorably learn new things through interacting, and integrating with American culture's diverse nature helped her pass through the odds to see the light at the end of the tunnel. It's what she suggests every newbie does when immersing in a newer environment—be open-minded, use the support system out there, and continue to learn new things.

One major trait the two of us have in common is what made our journey relatively easier, which is being open to learning new things in a novel environment and culture. The book provides you all the toolkits and processes you need to religiously follow to make your cultural integration, feasible, fast, and fun.

Yonas B. Keleta, PhD
Associate professor of Behavioral Neuroscience Research and Datamining Consultant

INTRODUCTION

How this Book Came About

I came to the United States of America full of confidence as I eagerly sought employment. I figured my English was fluent enough along with my BA in Sociology and Anthropology; I should find work in no time. So I was out to win with a big grin! I had no idea that I was going to be in for the shock of my life. It seemed as though the education I had worked hard to acquire was not recognized, or so I thought. Although I felt my English was reliable, it paled in comparison to the lack of cultural knowledge I needed to navigate the complexity that lay before me in my new culture. But I didn't let that stop me. I encourage you, the reader, to do just what I did—learn new things daily. It helps to develop your ability to work through the unfamiliar.

Although my command of English was good, an ocean of cultural knowledge lay before me, and it was complex to navigate. It took five years to have a sense of the whole culture.

Even today, after eleven years, I still find something new to learn every day. However, now it doesn't throw me off because I have developed skills to help me navigate how to handle what I don't know and the unfamiliar, and how to keep building on what I know.

In my struggle with learning this complex culture and developing some skills to navigate it, I often wondered if others were like me. Were other people, who left their native country to come to the US, going through difficulties of integrating into a new culture, or was this unique to me?

Or why haven't I met more people like me, sharing sadness and frustrations with empathetic friends? Where were those who had done this before? Why didn't they leave a way to make this process easier for the rest of us?

I can tell you I am a reader; ever since I read Pinocchio in Amharic (Ethiopia language) when I was seven, I was hooked for life. Up to the age of 18, I was a fiction junkie and read all the books I could put my hands on. Then all of a sudden, my interest shifted to non-fiction, mostly self-development books. I have read thousands of them. People who knew how I loved reading predicted I would be a writer one day. Many urged me to write. I also love to write. It's therapeutic for me to write. My diaries can attest to this. But it wasn't until this book that I decided to share my writing with others while remaining a reader.

I was telling you how I was wondering if anyone was going through the same thing, and if so, why didn't they leave a manual or instructions or the like?

I read a lot of books on American culture, history, and cultural integration, but to me, they lacked reproducible examples of how to gain skills and then apply them as it pertained to living in the Western world.

Despite feeling like a lost lamb at times, I was able to find friends and resources with useful information. I communicated with nonprofit organizations that work with immigrants to find medical and mental resources, US degree evaluation, housing, how-to fill out forms like job applications, etc.

The resources were excellent and helpful, and I continued to build my knowledge as I worked and volunteered for nonprofits to help new immigrants access the same kind of resources. However, to navigate the complexities that a new culture presented was challenging.

Luckily for me, I have always been a resourceful person without even knowing it. I pulled all the support I needed from wonderful friends who have supported me throughout the painful process. Such as counselors who guided me in understanding what was going on with me, people I encountered who made a difference in my life, and books and self-help programs that educated me about how to navigate cultures.

It took five years to understand what I was dealing with because my resources were scattered, and I had to put the puzzle together all on my own. And it would take me another two to three years to develop the skills necessary to help me navigate the complexity of the US culture, but through a lot of struggle and hard work, I finally got it. I was finally able to get my head above water to see what lay ahead of me. I will never forget that feeling of clarity and relief that came with it. And I was ready for my American dreams. I had different things I wanted to achieve, one of them being this book. I decided to compile everything I learned and leave a trail for others who come after me so that they don't have to struggle and wonder as I did.

One day I met Saliem, who struggled with integrating into the US culture for many years. Ultimately, this struggle cost her her life, which had a profound impact on me and gave me the push needed to share this book sooner than later.

I have worked many jobs in the USA, and I have met many immigrants that came to the US long ago. It was telling to hear them share their confusion, stresses, frustrations, and how similar their stories were to my own.

I started encouraging and coaching newcomers for free and have gotten a lot of feedback. I have heard many compliments, and what all of them had in common was that they never talked to someone who knew what they were talking about and had experienced similar situations. It finally hit me: it's not that people didn't go through the same path; they did, we all did, be it an immigrant, refugee, an asylee. The degree of the confusion might differ, but we all went through the same difficulty. However, for some reason, we tend to tell people, "don't worry, you will understand once you get into the system." When I was a newcomer, I hated hearing that sentence because I didn't understand what it meant. It would have been more helpful to hear someone share with me their experience, to see how to overcome similar struggles. Unfortunately, none of that was available to me. Don't get me wrong; I had great friends who supported me tremendously, but not in the way I mentioned. Sharing their experience with me would have given me quicker access to see what I was dealing with and identify what stage in the process I was on and how to deal with it. I searched for books and programs designed to help me with my struggles, and there were none.

It became apparent that life is what we make it to be, and if there is no way, make a way. It was time to give birth to this book.

Who Should Read This Book

Although I wrote this book about life experience in the USA, it will be useful for anyone who has left home for any reason and moved to another country to live permanently. Although I talk about integration to the US culture, the tools given here will be valuable to anyone who is building their home in a different place than their place of origin.

- If you have moved to another country for work and have to live there for quite some time, your challenges may be different than if you move permanently. However, you will find value in this book on a social aspect. If you want to know how to make real connections and strengthen your social support with locals, you will find this book helpful.
- If you plan to move to a new country, especially a western country, to make a life for yourself, the book will be an excellent resource for you to see what skills you need to work on before you make your move.

I wish I knew the depths of this book before I left my home country. I would have been better prepared, and I could have saved myself a lot of heartaches, and it would have given me a head start.

- I especially hope this book will be helpful for people in refugee camps who are waiting to go to the country chosen for them. I have met refugees through my job over the years; the reaction to being in the US is always the same. They feel like they waited five to seven years and sometimes ten with high expectations that their waiting and struggles are over when they arrive at their destination. Sadly, after arrival, they realize their battle just began in a new way. I've seen tears, disappointments, and anger because of their illusion and not being prepared.

- Anyone working with refugees and asylees, such as a caseworker, resettlement case manager, or perhaps a teacher whose students are immigrants, will gain an understanding of the challenges 1st immigrants go through emotionally, financially, and spiritually. This book will help you connect with them better and address their issues in a new way to serve them better.

I hope this book is a gift to everyone who reads it. May you find value in it.

How to Read This Book

It takes courage to even think about leaving home to live in another country. Then it takes bravery to plan the whole thing out and more bravery and courage is required to actually move. The anxiety that comes with it, the culture shock, the confusion, and the toll of starting over drives us to question our mental health at times. We all go through this and it's normal.

Please note, I am not a mental health professional, and this book should not be used as a replacement for mental health services.

You're in America - Now What? addresses how to recognize some of the challenges you will face the first year of arriving in the US and the years that follow, especially if you're coming from a developing country. I use my experiences and the wisdom of many other people whose stories I share throughout the book.

You will also discover:

- You're not alone in the process
- Tools to overcome difficult challenges and mental health issues with the process of cultural integration
- How to identify, create, and apply positive tools to help you through the tough times
- How to not feel like an outsider, but find your new home, find a sense of belonging, and fall in love with America without forgetting your birth country
- How to become empowered in your life and empower others
- How to bridge your knowledge of America and the country you left behind
- Learn what cultural integration is, develop the right attitude, learn the steps needed to help you survive integration and thrive in your new country, America

To Get the Best Out of This Book

1. I advise you to use the same bravery and courage it took to leave your native land; read this book and be open-minded and excited about your new discovery.

2. Allow information to flow in; empty your mind. Put aside everything you know and you have learned and read this with an adventurous spirit; you can pick up what you already know later after you finish reading this book. Take what you need from this book and leave what you don't think you need.

3. When you read about mental health, don't be afraid of the negative connotations that may have come from your culture. Welcome the idea of "mental health." In some cultures, whenever mental health is mentioned, we feel like someone is saying we are crazy. I think this is a false belief that we should unpack and throw away. Before you begin reading, I suggest being willing to let go of what you know and have been taught about mental health and be open to learning anew. It is important to understand mental health to take good care of it either with or without consulting a mental health professional. When I suggest checking your mental health, I am simply showing you what it takes to be strong in your mind and soul so you can handle your life in your new home country, the USA.

Disclaimers:

This book is a work of nonfiction. Real names have been used with permission and in some instances fictitious names have been used for privacy purposes.

The words, "The Immigrant" the author is referring to people who came to the USA as refugees, asylees, or any other status to eventually live as Americans.

The author is not a mental health professional. She is sharing her mental health experience and it should not be used as a replacement for care from a mental health care professional.

CHAPTER 1

WELCOME HOME

My hands were shaky and wet as I stood at the port of entry into the United States in San Francisco, California. I had seen this city in various movies, and I couldn't believe I was standing in San Francisco touching the ground. "Oh my God! I must be dreaming! Finally, I have arrived!" I had traveled for nearly 24 hours. I stayed overnight in Doha, Qatar and I was physically and mentally drained from the flight, sitting for a long time. My body's internal clock was out of sync with cues from the new time zone, and I felt a bit disoriented. However, I didn't care. I was too excited!

Traveling to the US, I spent a month in Kenya away from my country and family to process my visa. After several visits to the US Embassy, going through different health examinations, vaccines, enduring a lot of anxiety and fear of rejection, I was finally here.

It was exactly ten months since I received the first congratulations letter from the United States Citizenship and Immigration Services (USCIS), letting me know I had won the green card lottery for 2007. They asked me to complete a few long-form pages and identify a sponsor who lived in the US. I was skeptical and checked with my friend, Barbara who worked for the US Embassy in Asmara, the capital city of Eritrea, and asked her if it was legitimate. She confirmed that it was, giving me a huge smile. She was an American who worked as a nurse in the US Embassy. Barbara said to me, "if anyone deserves to be in America, it is you," knowing my circumstances. I was flattered, of course.

Aaron, my three-year-old son, was diagnosed with cerebral palsy, and I was just back in Asmara after being in China for a two year-long medical treatment for him. I had just begun working at the United Nations and was doing well financially. However, I worried about the future of Aaron and spoke about it often. So much so, one of my friends, Fanus, took me to an internet cafe to fill out the forms for a green card. I remember resisting, saying, "you've tried every year for the last ten years; what makes you think I can win this lottery when you did not?" Fanus ignored my pessimistic remarks and said, "we're doing it, and there is nothing you can do about it. You have nothing to lose by trying your luck." Sometimes our friends act like angels, and I am always grateful for Fanus, who was persistent and wouldn't take no for an answer.

The USCIS forms were long and challenging to complete, and most of the information I didn't understand. I had to identify a sponsor who lived in the US. The sponsor would be responsible for me until I was employed in the USA. With the help of dear friends, I raised money to pay the $750 visa fee plus the money for my travel to a neighboring country since Eritrea wasn't processing US visas at a time, so I had to travel to Kenya.

Although I don't recall the cost of my flight, I remember it was quite pricey. Plus, my expenses for health check-ups and vaccines and month-long expenditures in Kenya. I stayed with a very generous Irish priest and friend to keep the costs low. And after ten months of toiling in Asmara, Kenya, spending approximately $10,000, hours and hours of planning, sleepless nights, desperation, and anxiety, I was finally standing in San Francisco. My reward for all the hard work had paid off. I was proud!

My emotions ran rapidly from crying to laughing, feeling numb, excited, nostalgic, fearful, and anxious. I couldn't keep one feeling in one place for longer than a few minutes. I did it! What was once impossible was actually possible and happening. I looked up to the heavens and said my gratitude.

My sponsor, Taame's daughter, Semira, who I call my cousin, although we are family friends, picked me up at the San Francisco airport. It was a chilly night. I shivered several times; luckily for me, she grabbed a jacket for me. With everything going on, I didn't think about checking the weather. I thanked Semira for being so thoughtful.

She took me to a party at her friend's home in San Francisco before heading home. I remember people were excited to see a new person arriving from Africa. They complimented me on how great my language skill was. They made me laugh comparing my English with someone who moved to the US ten years prior, which made me feel good about my ability to communicate. I am sure they said, "Welcome to America." After leaving the party, we went to my temporary home in San Jose, California, an hour or so drive.

I am sure I heard the words "Welcome to America" several times over the days. Over the days that followed. Relatives of my sponsor streamed in to welcome me and wish me well.

My luggage was delayed and ended up in Europe. I was upset because every change of clothes I had was in there. People who came to welcome me were very generous. They gave me a few hundred dollars to buy clothes. Uncle Teame, who is on my father's side, that I had never met, came to see me and gave me money to buy clothes and a blanket. Another relative came with a blanket, pillows, and towels, which I felt was thoughtful. Not that my sponsor didn't provide me with all those things, but because they were thinking ahead, for when I became independent enough to leave my sponsor's house, those were basic things I would need.

Despite all the generosity and welcoming I received, I didn't feel at home. I was anxious to get a job. I felt under pressure to get busy, save money, and send for Aaron, who was to join me in six months. My dad would accompany him. Before I moved, the US Embassy informed me that my son was entitled to come with me. However, I had to apply for a visa and take him with me; if not, I would have six months to get him to the USA after I was in America. If I couldn't get him to the USA within six months, his visa would expire, and I wouldn't be able to apply for a visa for him until having been a USA citizen for five years.

I decided to leave Aaron home to come to the US first and prepare for his basic needs. I was always nervous and toiling and couldn't even enjoy simple things because of the pressure of wanting to get my son to the US in such a short time. I felt bombarded by the fast-paced

4

way of American life. It seemed everyone spoke fast, ate fast, and walked fast as if everything was on speed dial. I had started to wonder if I made a mistake coming to the USA and if finding a job in the United Nations somewhere else, preferably in a developing country or Europe, would have been better.

However, although I struggled and didn't like what I was going through, I knew it was the right country for Aaron and me because of the many services he needed. It was three or four years before I felt welcomed in the United States. My dear pen pal, Bill, who lived in Germany at a time, introduced me to Troy, his nephew, who was born and grew up in California. Sometimes you don't know why you meet people right away. He was a veteran and had served in Afghanistan. We discovered we had a lot to talk about since I had previous army training experience in Africa. Our meetings were always long and exciting. We called each other brother and sister. We both recognized the similarities in our behaviors and how we felt about the world.

It was surprising that someone born and raised in a different country would have as many similarities of experiences, thoughts, and beliefs as I did. It was my first real connection with an American; although I had met many Americans before that, this connection was different.

One day, Troy took me to a nearby hiking area when I told him repeatedly that I was feeling overwhelmed. Although I loved hiking back home, I hadn't even thought about going hiking up until that point. I didn't even know where to go because I was always living in survival mode and having fun or taking time for myself wasn't on my calendar.

After we drove for 20 minutes, entering the redwoods, I was stunned and mesmerized by the magnificent trees and the energy I felt around nature. It was such a difference from being bombarded by the big city and fast-paced life. Troy said, "you can retreat to the woods and away from the city when you feel stressed." I nodded my head in agreement. I felt like I was at home. I couldn't explain it; however, for the first time, in the woods, embraced by nature, I felt at home. Intuitively understanding what I was feeling, Troy told me some of the trees were as old as 2000 years, and the energy I felt was normal.

He sat me near one of the aged trees and said, "Senait, I know you are going through a lot right now. I want you to know that you are doing an amazing job with your son. We are a culture stuck in chasing money. We value possession, and we are losing our time to connect with ourselves. No one has time for anyone, and real connection is not so easy to find here. Just know this is the country you came to, and there is also a lot of beauty around you if you look close enough. America is so lucky to have you, with all your wisdom and love for people. I want to welcome you to your home. It is my home, my ancestor's land, and I want to welcome you. "Welcome Home!"

Troy hugged me as a brother or a father would have. He is a very spiritual person who was influenced by the Native American way of life. I couldn't help but cry with joy as I felt welcomed for the first time, by him and by the land, the trees, and the air. I felt it! My God, I am home!

I welcome you, readers, to the USA, similarly, as I was welcomed. I know you heard it many times from people, if you haven't felt it

6

because those words were rushed and didn't sink in, I want to welcome you to your home! It doesn't matter how you got here. You may have come to the USA by winning a green card lottery as I did, maybe as a refugee or asylees, or you married a US citizen, or you came for work. It doesn't matter how you got here, welcome home!

Welcome even if you have lived here for four or five years or more and never felt welcomed. Thank you for your bravery and courage to leave everything familiar and jump into the unknown. Not everyone is willing to do that. Thank you for coming to the USA, trusting that we Americans and its land are worth what you sacrificed.

Thank you for bringing all your love, new perspectives, new dreams, creativity, family, faith, and everything that you are. We Americans are a better nation because of people like you. Welcome, and America promises that you will find every dream possible, and I know if you are focused and work hard, you will achieve all the goals you came to accomplish in America.

You inherit a country that, at times, will feel divided. Some Americans are racists, bitter, not welcoming; some people will test you and not be friendly. Some will be impatient. You will discover some things against your belief and values, and some people will try to manipulate you, even use you.

I want you to understand that America isn't heaven and there is bad behavior like you would find anywhere in the world. And more than ever, you might feel frightened, unwelcome, and intimidated. It's understandable. Know that the racial tension that exists today is shocking to many US citizens as well. There is nothing you need to do about that but remember that circumstances don't last forever. Instead of berating yourself, blaming others, or acting irrationally, use your energy to acknowledge the truth.

Step into more courage for proactively changing your life. Focus instead on a new and exciting project that will improve your enjoyment of life and give you something you did not have before. Focus on the positive and the positive people you meet who are willing to help you adjust.

I know many Americans—social workers—mental health professionals—doctors—caseworkers—who have never traveled to other countries. Still, they are so wise because of their interaction with immigrants, place themselves in immigrants' shoes, and empathize with what the experience might feel like for you.

I love this story I heard when I first moved to the USA. Every time I hear this story, it always reminds me of where my focus should be. Here is how the story goes:

An old Cherokee is teaching his grandson about life.

"A fight is going on inside me," he said to the boy. "It is a terrible fight, and it is between two wolves. One is evil—he is anger, envy, sorrow, regret, greed, arrogance, self-pity, guilt, resentment, inferiority, lies, false pride, superiority, and ego." He continued, "The other is good—he is joy, peace, love, hope, serenity, humility, kindness, benevolence, empathy, generosity, truth, compassion, and faith. The same fight is going on inside you–and inside every other person, too." The grandson thought about it for a minute and then asked his grandfather: "Which wolf will win?" The old Cherokee simply replied, "The one you feed."

The moral of the story is simple. As immigrants, we have two conflicting selves within us. One comes out of frustration; it tells us America isn't what you thought it was, you wish you could go back, hate how certain people treat and view you, and hate the struggle you are having with surviving. You might question, "Why is my neighbor looking at me strangely?" Your thoughts might overreact and think, "Americans are racist, America is an awful place, people are not friendly, the language is so difficult, and I don't think I can ever learn it. If people are not going to be helpful, I will just stick to my community who speaks my language and understands my ways."

You refuse to learn more and how to survive on a bigger scale no matter how many years you live in the USA. You complain to people how busy and boring America is; worry about your children not learning your culture. They are becoming Americans without manners; you even think about moving them back to your country of origin.

The other side of you feels momentarily happy when you see your social worker helping you, or you:

- meet a kind person who is so curious about your origin country
- meet someone who makes you completely welcome
- feel inspired, eager to learn new things, and anxious to discover new things about yourself
- get curious about keeping your values and accepting the benefits of America

- read a book on how to connect with Americans and make friends
- are not afraid when your kids bring their friends who are not from your culture, you welcome them and even learn from them
- work hard with a goal in mind, and you understand at the end that hard work is your dream job, your dream car, your dream home, your dream community, your American dream that you came to achieve.

So which wolf is going to win? Like the old Cherokee said, "the one you feed." Keep on reading, and I will show you how you can feel empowered in the US as an immigrant despite all that is going on around you and along the way, and by the end of the book, you will learn which wolf you need to feed to achieve your American dream. It's an honor to serve you!

What is Cultural Integration?

This chapter is a significant one. I think it is essential for you to understand what culture is and how it is acquired, and once you know that, it will be easy for you to understand why cultural integration is difficult and tends to take a lot of time.

Sociology defines culture as a particular society with its own beliefs, knowledge, values, behaviors, customs, ways of life, art, etc., that bind people together.

Values help shape a society by suggesting what is right and wrong, beautiful and ugly, sought or avoided. Values are culture's standard for discerning what is reasonable and just in society. They are deeply embedded and critical for transmitting and teaching a culture's beliefs.

> *Beliefs are the insets or convictions that people hold to be true. Individuals in a society have specific views, but they also share collective values. To illustrate the difference, Americans commonly believe that anyone who works hard enough will be successful and wealthy in the American dream. Underlying this belief is the American value that wealth is useful and important.*
>
> *(Source: Introduction to Sociology; OpenStax CNX)*

We will get technical here, and it might be boring, but I promise to give you examples to keep it understandable. I will try to pinpoint how this relates to your experience, so keep reading. I think it is essential for you to understand what culture is and how it is acquired. It lays the foundation, and once you know, it will be easy for you to understand why cultural integration might be difficult and tends to take time.

Living up to a culture's values can be difficult. It's easy to value good health, but it's hard to quit smoking. Marital monogamy is appreciated, but many spouses engage in infidelity. Cultural diversity and equal opportunities for all people are valued in the United States, yet white men have dominated the country's highest political offices. That is why you see the Black Lives Matter movement trying to move America to its values, "that all people are equal."

YOU'RE IN AMERICA — *NOW WHAT?*

One way societies strive to put values into action is through rewards, sanctions, and punishments. When people observe the norms of society and uphold their values, they're often rewarded.
(Source: Introduction to Sociology 2e. OpenStax CNX)

When people go against a society's values, they are punished by society. I remember as a young person, when we rode the bus, how when an elderly person got on, if I was still seated, all eyes landed on me in disapproval, implying that I should give up my seat. No need for words, it's understood, a form of societal punishment.

In the same scenario, if I had seen the elderly woman right away when she got on, and I got up and guided her to sit where I was seated, the look on everyone would be one of approval, smile, nod and sometimes people would say, "bless you." It was a cultural reward.

In a similar example as above, if this happened in the USA, I bet someone would call and report me, which would fall into a sanction.

Values are not static; they vary across time and between groups as people evaluate, debate, and change collective societal beliefs. Values also differ from culture to culture. For example, cultures differ in their values about what kinds of physical closeness are appropriate in public. It's rare to see two male friends or co-workers holding hands in the United States, where that behavior often symbolizes romantic feelings. But in many nations, masculine physical intimacy is considered natural in public.
Source: (Introduction to Sociology 2e. OpenStax CNX)

I remember an experience my girlfriend and I had for many years when we were new to the US culture. We are both heterosexuals, affectionate with one another platonically. As we were walking, I had my arm around her shoulder, and one person passed us with a look of disapproval; another called us "a cute couple" and nodded in approval. We were stunned and uncomfortable.

In our country, the reaction we would have received from people was no attention at all most of the time, and sometimes a smile, a nod, and sometimes followed by a question like "you guys look so happy, how long have you been friends?" And no one would assume we are romantically involved.

At that point, I understood why my new American friend felt uncomfortable when I hugged her and put my arms around her shoulders when we walked. It took me years to learn to give my friends their personal space and work out a way to ask permission if it's ok to hug them if they need comfort since I am a hugger. However, I stopped holding people's hands unless it was my husband or my kids. One's ethical values in one culture could suggest wrong meaning in another.

All these examples describe the visible and invisible rules of conduct through which societies are structured or what sociologists call norms.

A norm is *how to behave by what society has defined as good, right, and important, and most members of the society adhere to them.*

Formal norms are established written rules. Those are punishable by law if you don't follow them. For example, in the USA, driving under the influence of alcohol is punishable by law. This same act might not be punishable by law in another country. I find many people in the courthouse charged for this crime with a look of stunned disbelief on their faces, and I often hear them say the same thing although the defendants don't know each other. "But I only had a few beers; what is the problem?" In their culture, it isn't a big deal.

However, formal norms are quickly learned because they are written laws.

How about informal norms? *Open Education Sociology Dictionary defines informal norms as a casual behavior to which an individual generally conforms. People learn informal norms by observation, imitation, and general socialization. Some informal norms are taught directly—"Kiss your Aunt Edna" or "Use your napkin"—while others are learned by observation, including observations of the consequences when someone else violates a norm.*

Source: (Introduction to Sociology 2e. OpenStax CNX)

An excellent example of that is my Grandma Workuha. I remember when she moved in with us, I think I was 13 or 14. She came from a village to the city for the first time, where we lived in Addis Ababa, Ethiopia. While walking on the road, she was saying hello to everyone we passed by. People were looking at her funny and I was always embarrassed by her behavior. My mom and I told her that she didn't have to say hello to everyone she encounters, and we will never forget what she told us, "Are you crazy? I am not an animal. Even animals greet each other. How can I not greet everyone I meet?" We laughed. We told Grandmother that in the city, we didn't do that.

My grandmother continued to greet everyone she passed by every day. My God, it must have been exhausting for her compared to the village she came from, where everyone knows everyone by name. But we let her be, we knew she grew up with this value, and it was important to her, and she did this until she passed away in 2003.

So, you can imagine why moving to another country and adapting new ways, and going through successful cultural integration could be so challenging and confusing.

Sometimes this process could be a little easier when you have moved only far enough where language and culture are still different but not far from your country. There are existing familiar traits of the people that unite them, making the process easier. A typical example of that is moving within a continent or maybe even to a neighboring country. And please don't be mistaken in believing that this kind of move is easy. No, it comes with a lot of struggle as well, but it's relatively easier than when you move across your continent to a place where sometimes your cultural belief clashes with the new culture. You get confused about putting the two together to make integration possible and feel disoriented most of the time till you figure it all out, which might take years. We call that culture shock.

Dealing with Culture Shock

Wikipedia defines culture shock as an experience a person may have when one moves to a cultural environment which is different from one's own; it is also the personal disorientation a person may feel when experiencing an unfamiliar way of life due to immigration or a visit to a new country, a move between social environments, or simply transition to another type of life. One of the most common causes of culture shock involves individuals in a foreign environment. Culture shock can be described as consisting of at least one of four distinct phases: honeymoon, negotiation, adjustment, and adaptation.

If you have moved from a different cultural society as I did, you probably felt lost because all the values, norms, and coping skills you have learned up to that point might not serve you in your new country. And you realize the gap and learning you have to do to live in the new culture. That could be extremely frustrating. It's like asking someone to be a kid again. Most times, you might feel like a kid who doesn't know what the adults around are talking about.

Learning the language is the first challenge, and understanding the law is the next, and the most challenging is learning the informal norms. How do you know something that is not written or spoken? It's usually by observation.

As kids, we had no problem because we observed and learned. We made a mistake, and society is more forgiving towards kids, so no problem even if you get slapped here or there. However, as adults, the constant shaming look and disapproval from people who don't know anything about you can increase your anxiety level. Often, you might not know what you did. How do you learn those norms and be part of the culture that embraces you and creates a sense of belonging?

My first cultural shock happened when my parents decided to move to Eritrea. It was about an hour flight from Addis Ababa (Ethiopia). It was a move within the same continent. I was around 16 and was so sad I had to leave everything behind. I questioned why we had to move to a country we didn't know, and I gave my family a hard time when I decided to hide and disappear for the whole day. I didn't want to go to a country I didn't know, leaving everything behind. My family told me they moved to Ethiopia for a better lifestyle before my siblings and I were born, and now it was time to go back to their country after it had gained independence. Although I never been there, they said that was where I was from, and it was my parent's final decision. I had no choice but to go with them.

I remember I made the whole experience so difficult for my parents at the airport, on the flight, and for the next six months. I was sad, and my parents had a hard time getting a single smile out of me.

To make matters worse, although I spoke the language a little bit with a heavy accent, I was made fun of by kids my age, nothing I did was right, I felt shame, I felt people's wrath when I did something outside of the cultural norm. I had people yell at me until they heard my accent, then they calmed a little bit and would say, "still, your parents should teach you better." They didn't understand the culture I came from, so they expected me to understand the Eritrean cultural values as if it is the only value people in the world practiced.

At school, I felt isolated and confused. I finally found kids like me who also moved to Eritrea from Ethiopia after Eritrea's independence.

I remember we refused to hang out with kids that were born and grew up in Eritrea. They called us names, and we did the same in return.

For about five years, I made sure I stayed within a community we created for ourselves. I had more and more friends, only those who came from Addis. We always talked about how wrong the other kids were, how incorrect the culture was, and how unfair everything was, including how they spoke. We only thought we knew better.

I really don't know how it happened, but we started getting to know the local kids, and integration occurred slowly but surely. There were still bumps in cultural clashes here and there, but we were integrating slowly. Our private graduation picnic circle included two girls originally from Addis and five locals we connected with and considered friends.

After completing the 12th grade, we were sent far from home to a harsh environment for military training (National service) as it was the country's way. We were to stay there and wait for our matriculation exam, which wasn't for another three months. It was a harsh situation designed to teach us to overcome hardship. Two of my friends were with me, in the same division and hut. Yes, we stayed in a big hut, it's a long story and more about that later. The food was dreadful, but we brought peanut butter, jelly, crackers, and some other power food to help us get through the six months.

I started sharing my food with my two friends, and after we ate mine, I expected my friends would share theirs. Instead, they were hiding theirs. I came from a culture where sharing was a must. They were not. The first time I caught one of my friends eating and hiding

18

from me, I felt like a "deer in headlights" I couldn't say anything. I left without saying a word, and that was the end of our relationship. No conversation and no confrontation. Looking back, I must admit I didn't understand it at the time as a culture shock.

I felt betrayed. I got mad and talked about her to my new friends in another division, and they couldn't believe it either. Long story short, someone I once considered a friend quickly became an adversary.

Later, I discovered that friend grew up in a country always going through war. Everything was uncertain, being frugal and careful with food was a survival skill she acquired from her experience. She was never trying to hurt me.

Like me, you may have had a culture shock that caused a relationship to end, thinking the person is horrible and wrong. It's normal. Being in a new situation for the first time, you often don't know how to handle it.

In this book, we will look at different tools to help you cope with similar situations that may save friendships.

The first tool I will give you in this chapter on how to handle cultural shock is:

Evaluate Your Beliefs

Just because the culture you came from did things, talked in a certain way, and has values that you are accustomed to, it doesn't mean that is the truth for everyone else. You may be scratching your head right about now, which is okay. I did the same thing when I heard this for the first time. We are not alone. Talk to any religious person, and they will tell you theirs is the only true religion. I want you to have the idea that we, human beings, childishly think we are right, ours is the only truth, our culture is the only superior culture, our religion is the only true religion, and so on and so on. We are all guilty of this. The trick is to use every experience exposed to you, evaluate your long-held beliefs, and be willing to change them if you discover they are not valid.

To give you a little background, I don't remember my first culture shock in China, but it was one culture shock after another consistently for the first three months. I wasn't sure I liked being there, most of my experience made me super uncomfortable, and I wanted to go back home.

I felt nostalgic. I wanted the street I walked on to smell like home; I wanted the people I passed to be familiar to me. However, China wasn't familiar. The streets smelled different. (I didn't know streets have a unique smell before that!) The people had odors I wasn't used to; the food was different, with unusual flavors I didn't know or recognize; and all five of my senses were overwhelmed, not understanding what they were experiencing.

Circumstances forced me to stay longer, and I got a job as an English as a second language teacher. Slowly, I started getting used to the kids, started making friends, and was okay with staying. I began to be curious about a lot of things, especially their culture.

Let's look at two examples from my experience to elaborate my point:

Example #1

One day, I had a disturbing dream the previous night, which involved blood and me being chased and stabbed. That morning, one of my assistant Chinese teachers noticed I looked concerned and wasn't my usual joyful persona. I walked like a zombie with a worried look on my face. She asked what was bothering me. I hesitated, weighing the nature of our formal relationship, but finally, I gave in to her persistent concern and told her about my dream. She looked puzzled and said, "So why are you concerned? It is indeed a beautiful dream. Red is a sign of good luck, and good luck is going to find you."

Wait? What? That was my reaction. Although she succeeded in making me feel a bit more relaxed, why wasn't she taking this seriously? Because in my culture, red in a dream means danger, or so I thought. But she explained that red is for luck, joy, and happiness, be it in a dream or awake. She said that is why they use red colors for everything on their holidays, and even their flag is red.

I didn't know which perspective to choose for quite some time since red had quite the opposite meaning in my culture than the culture I was trying to adapt to. It was a massive moment for me to stop and realize that I felt like making my culture right and the Chinese culture wrong. And for my Chinese colleague, she felt puzzled why my Culture was interpreting it wrong. The same dream with two different cultural interpretations. It was a natural reaction for both of us.

However, this was also the first time I saw an opportunity to reevaluate long-held beliefs. Maybe, if we asked another person from

Europe, they might have told us a different meaning of the dream. And better yet, for someone else, dreams are just dreamed with no definitions at all. This realization was both scary and liberating at the same time. It was scary. I felt like I was betraying my culture. It was liberating because now I could choose which dream interpretation I wanted to believe in the future.

Our cultural conditioning happens at an early age. We hold so many beliefs that we think are true, and that's why we should use moments of culture shock to be open to what's unfamiliar to us and reevaluate our beliefs. Although the need to judge the new cultural belief is strong, be open to the unfamiliar.

In this example, I chose to reevaluate a belief I thought was correct, which gave me a choice. A choice to continue to believe that seeing blood in a dream means danger or to think, as Chinese do, that blood is good luck.

After thinking about it for some time, I decided to choose that seeing blood in one's dream means good luck just because it made me feel better. Knowing that if I had decided that seeing blood means danger or that it doesn't mean anything, it would also be okay.

After I went back home and checked with people about this belief, I found out not everyone in my culture agreed with my original interpretation. Some believed blood in a dream meant good luck. Go figure!

If I didn't choose to evaluate the beliefs I had, my reaction would have been: "My God, what is she talking about? Doesn't she know blood is the sign of danger, and that is the truth and nothing but the truth? She is wrong, and she doesn't even know it." I might have tried to convince her of my truth. Or I might have thought, "What is the point? She will not understand. This culture is weird. What kind of culture did I come to live in? I don't belong here; I need to find some other foreigners, make friends, and avoid Chinese people altogether."

The latter reaction is how most of us react, and it's a standard defense mechanism. We feel obligated to defend our beliefs with all we've got. This kind of reaction will keep us isolated, and we would never discover the beauty and rich culture of the new country.

Choose not to judge another's culture because you might not have enough information to understand that culture's traditions.

Besides, judging will only make you feel bad because you will always feel like complaining. You don't have time to complain. Complaining and a negative state of mind robs you from experiencing your positive energy, which is an essential tool for you to tackle what lies ahead of you.

Whenever you encounter a culture shock, having a non-judgmental attitude, being honest with yourself, being curious, accepting what is, and having a sense of humor helps!

If I were born and grew up in China, I would adopt the same belief, the same culture, and the same dream interpretation, different from the country I was born and grew up in. It tells us that we are conditioned to believe in a certain way according to where we were born and grew up. We learn belief systems. We learn skills that we need to survive in that environment, and those are important because we survived our environments with the skills and beliefs we learned.

Now that we are in America, we have to revise those beliefs as they come up. Not all beliefs and views are useful, and not all are to our advantage when we move to another culture. It doesn't mean, however, that we throw our values out the door.

Example # 2

While in China, I met another new friend, Victoria, through a mutual friend. Our friendship was blossoming, and I was getting invited to her house for drinks and visits with her family. One day she said, "Senait, I want to ask you something." I said, "Sure, anything!"

"My family and I are wondering whether your darkness was natural? If you take a shower, does your skin get lighter?" I was shocked and offended by her simple sounding question. I felt as if my blood was boiling, and my stomach and jaws were tightening. How dare they invite me to their home to insult me. In my mind, I was forming all kinds of comeback insults. But before I could say anything, I noticed her facial expression as she waited on my answer. It was the same expression that my students gave me when they asked an innocent question. I was puzzled; I asked her to repeat the question. She repeated it, and this time I also noticed her tone was also like my students when they were curious. That softened me up. What was happening? Later I would learn, Victoria and her family had this burning question in their heads but never were close enough to anyone of color to ask the question. I also knew China was a closed country to the rest of the world for so long, seeing foreigners wasn't usual.

24

I stepped away from feeling offended, and I searched for answers to reply to her question. I responded, "Listen, I know you are not coming from a place to hurt me, and you are curious, but I want to tell you that I am a bit offended about this question. However, because I know you didn't mean anything by it and wanted to know with all your honesty, I will also meet you where you are." Victoria sounded puzzled and apologized over and over again. I told her not to worry about it because she didn't even know what she was apologizing for. I shared with her what I told my Chinese students when they asked me why I was black. It often happened whenever I went into a new classroom. I knew her family had three adorable kittens, black and orange. I asked her if she bathes all three kittens. She said, "of course."

"After you wash all of them, does the black one change color to something else?" Victoria screamed! A light bulb went on, and she realized how offensive her question was, although she meant it with all sincerity in her heart. Victoria apologized again with an understanding of the heaviness and silliness of her question. She said she didn't know the origin of her family's belief about black people.

Maybe they don't take showers because there is a lack of water, or they get dark in the sun and wonder if the darkness goes away when taking a shower. Once Victoria got it, she told me that she was glad I was patient with her childish curiosity and false belief. I told her that was fine.

That day, Victoria was relieved of her false belief about black people. Not only related to showers and the sun, but the need to question why anyone is black.

Victoria got that if she doesn't ever wonder why her kitten is black, she had no business asking black people why they were black. I saw her smile with relief, a little bit embarrassed, and rid her of the false belief right then. That day freed me from my false belief and judgment that Chinese people are very racist.

It helped that I chose to remain calm and see her innocent question instead of thinking how offensive it was, but she did the work in freeing herself from her false belief. What if she had held on to her belief and said something like, "But those kittens are not people, it's not the same thing," arrogantly defending her opinion. Then that friendship would have ended right then. Victoria would have always held that belief and offended other black friends she might have found on her way. But she chose to consider her belief for what it was, false and not the truth. Victoria also acknowledged her error and let it go. We maintained our friendship, and Victoria kept telling people what she discovered.

As I mentioned above, her willingness to observe the false belief and free herself in front of me also freed me from my belief that I was holding against Chinese people since I arrived there. I thought Chinese people were rude, noisy, had no respect, and were very racist. Until my students and Victoria helped me understand that I misunderstood their curiosity for all the characteristics I mentioned above. There may have been some racist comments here and there, but they were all willing to see through the ignorance they held, so I was able to free myself from the ignorant belief I had about them from the short time I had been there.

However, it doesn't mean there are no racist people in China. As a matter of fact, I met many of them; all I am saying is that I was holding a false belief all Chinese were racist, which was wrong. Without all the false thoughts clouding my judgment, I started to explore China's wonders, their beautiful culture and art. Honestly, I completely fell in love with the cultural aspects of China. When I left after two years, I left richer in thoughts and perspective than when I arrived, and with many friendships I cherished.

It's easy to get offended and fight for what we believe in without questioning if it is true. We all do it at times, but it's always good to evaluate our beliefs and judgments. After all, we were fed our culture's beliefs when we were kids or during an experience we didn't understand like in the above example.

When we were kids, we had no choice but to believe what we learned from our culture, and we all agree all cultures have excellent and wrong beliefs and practices. However, as adults, we are in a position to question what we have learned. We can keep what we value and discard what we don't think we need, what is false, and what doesn't serve us anymore.

In a way, your move from your country of origin to a completely different culture is a gift. Once again, you get to be like a child to question everything, free from what you have learned for many years, and now you can sort them out and look at them and choose for yourself whether a particular belief or skill is useful. You are not your beliefs. You are more than that. You are full of potential, capable of learning anything at any time and any age. Unload and unpack your luggage of beliefs; you no longer need them in your present situation, like you discard clothes and shoes you outgrow.

Stages of Cultural Integration

The process of undoing or unlearning to learn new skills is a harrowing one. You are shedding and growing new skin. This process can be scary because once you put aside all your beliefs and skills you have acquired, what is left is pure potential. It's as if you were a child, and you have never been in that space till now, and you don't know what it is like to be there.

The amount of difficulty you experience depends on how willing you are in this process of undoing and unlearning. When I say undoing or unlearning, it doesn't mean you will discard everything you have believed and learned—far from it! But you don't identify who you are with your beliefs and set of skills any longer, and you can detach yourself from it all and observe what skills you want to keep and which skills you want to discard. You accept that your belief system is yours, and it isn't necessarily how the rest of the world sees your world. You respect your views, and at the same time, you are willing to see the world as others view it. Having both worldviews will help you increase your capability to solve problems faster and have a solid friendship with others not from your place of origin. Having that attitude also allows you to determine which beliefs you want to hold tightly and which to discard because they don't serve you anymore.

This book's purpose isn't to tell you which beliefs you need to discard or which ones to keep. The process is yours and yours alone.

No one can tell you what to do and what to believe. The blending of the two cultures within you (the country you left and your new country) can be an easy, fun process to make a new, unique you. Only if you stop following what others tell you, and dive deep to do the work yourself. No one knows yourself better than you.

If you have just arrived in the US, you have a lot of work ahead for the next five to ten years. This book aims to make that process faster and easier for you. Sometimes, you want to change your belief, but you see your community believes the same thing. Hence, you don't want to be the only one to let people know you no longer have a particular belief. You might want to live a different style, but you feel stuck: that is understandable since we want to be accepted in our communities, and we do that by maintaining the status quo and not rocking the boat.

If that is the case, you can still be part of a community of your choice, make changes within yourself, and become a bold leader to influence your community to change individual behaviors that you feel strongly about. This process requires you to develop the skills to be a community leader. We will discuss this in a later chapter.

I believe cultural integration is possible and accomplished with ease. Life can be successful by following proper instructions. Just like when you want to get your driver's license, you can study the driver's manual. After you have reviewed it and feel comfortable, you must take the learner's permit test before applying for your driver's license. In America, a learner's permit is required before obtaining a driver's license. After you have passed the learner's permit test, you are eligible to get behind a car with an instructor to learn the rules of the road.

Again, you must follow instructions to become a safe, skilled, and sage driver. See what learning something new can do . . . ?

If you want to be a US citizen, you must be prepared as well. I was at a library while writing this chapter, and what is fascinating is that there is a "citizenship corner" where people can come and find resources in US public libraries. Books, Ebooks, CDs and DVDs are available to help you prepare to pass your exam. They even have a volunteer teacher that comes to the libraries to help the testers. It is an excellent resource.

The same applies to integration; we need guidance to learn how to develop new skills. We need to learn how to navigate the US culture while learning how to integrate it. And now you have the tools in this book to help you integrate with ease. I share with you examples of some of the stages you will go through, give you examples and offer suggestions on managing the steps.

I want you to be prepared and pass the invisible exam of being integrated into US culture successfully. Take it seriously. It is as important as becoming a citizen. I planned this book to help you successfully deal with every immigration issue you will encounter.

Having a paper that says you are an American isn't enough to make you an American. You must completely immerse yourself in the US culture while also sharing your values and cultural values with your friends and community. I wish I had this book when I moved.

There are many books and resources to teach you about American values. However, I learned there was so much missing, and it validates why this book is the missing link. This book will save you years of confusion and research because I've done most of the work for you.

Now, let's look at the integration stage and the process to give you direction to locate where you are and what you need to do to integrate for a successful life. The process and stages of integration are explained differently; my favorite is by an intercultural development and communication expert, Dr. Milton Bennett.

He describes the model in a series of six stages, a continuum of attitudes toward cultural differences. The goal is to move from the *ethnocentric stages of denial, minimization, and to the ethnorelative stages of acceptance, adaptation, and integration.*

Bennett further describes ethnocentrism as *an attitude or mindset which presumes the superiority of one's worldview, sometimes without even acknowledging the existence of others. On the other hand, ethnorelativism assumes the equality and validity of all groups and does not judge others by the standards of one's own culture.* Bennett's six-stage model is summarized below.

Ethnocentrism Has Three Stages

Denial

People in the denial stage do not recognize the existence of cultural differences. They are completely ethnocentric in that they believe there is a correct type of living (theirs), and that those who behave differently simply don't know any better. In this phase, people are prone to imposing their value system upon others, believing that they are "right" and that others who are different are "confused."

They are not threatened by cultural differences because they refuse to accept them. Generally, those who experience cultural denial have not had extensive contact with people different from themselves and thus have no experiential basis for believing in other cultures. A key indicator of the denial stage is the belief that you know better than the locals.

Previously, I gave you an example of when I moved to Eritrea as a teenager and refused to accept the cultural difference. I wanted to make friends, but only with friends that were born in Ethiopia like me. I was trying to make the culture wrong, and I honestly believed something was wrong with all Eritrean people born there. I thought my belief system was the only way, and anything that didn't match was just entirely wrong. I was in the denial stage.

After reading this, you might realize you're in this stage. If this happens, don't worry, we all go through this stage, and there is nothing wrong here. I have met immigrants in this denial stage despite living here for more than twenty, thirty years. I have also met people born and raised in the USA at this stage, not wanting to accept another way of life other than what they know.

For some, this stage is the only reality, and they never learn there is a much better way.

Minimization

People in the minimization stage of ethnocentrism are still threatened by cultural differences and try to minimize them by telling themselves that people are more similar than dissimilar. No longer do they see those from other cultures as being misguided, inferior, or unfortunate. They still have not developed cultural self-awareness and are insistent about getting along with everyone. Because they assume that all cultures are fundamentally similar, people in this stage fail to tailor their approaches to a cultural context. This stage is a nice step forward from denial and defense—a glimpse of what is possible.

Defense

Those in the defense stage are no longer blissfully ignorant of other cultures; they recognize the existence of other cultures, but not their validity. They feel threatened by the presence of other ways of thinking and thus denigrate them to assert their own culture's superiority. Cultural differences are seen as problems to be overcome, and there is a dualistic "us vs. them" mentality. Whereas those in the denial stage are unthreatened by the presence of other cultural value systems (they don't believe in them, after all), those in the defense stage do feel threatened by "competing" cultures. People in the defense stage tend to surround themselves with members of their own culture and avoid contact with members from other cultures. This stage is a nice step forward from denial and defense—a glimpse of what is possible.

Some immigrants I met who belong in this category complain about America and the life they had hoped to achieve but never did. Although they are Americans on paper, they refused to see themselves as Americans. They reap the benefit of being here, but they still live their life the same way they were living in their home country.

They force and demand their children who were born in America not to marry outside of their race. In some severe cases, the parents demand them to marry someone from the village where their parents originated. There is no room for compromise. I have met several people born in the US, second-generation immigrants, that have cut off relationships with their parents because they wanted to marry someone outside of their nationality. In some cases, they lead a confused life, and some turn to alcohol and drugs or avoid marriage altogether.

Don't think even for a second that only immigrants find themselves in this stage. Even Americans who think America is only for them can be classified in this stage. With the Trump administration in power, people became more and more vocal about their beliefs regarding immigration. I have encountered some Americans who were born and grew up here who are in this stage. They feel threatened by outsiders coming and taking their jobs and changing their culture. I've seen comments on my city's public Facebook page, like "we don't want any immigrants here; we want to make America great again," and I was shocked to read something like that. It didn't make sense because it doesn't match the American value. However, as I mentioned above, when we talked about values, just because something is a common value, it doesn't mean everybody follows it.

What makes it sad is that with all the illegal immigration issues brewing in the country, you might hear people saying some nasty stuff like, "go back to where you came from," and that might make belonging difficult. I get it. It's where I need you to get thick skin because many people in the US don't believe that. The whole US is in shock, trying to handle the immigration issue. To make matters worse, the few Americans at this stage don't even know the difference between illegal and legal immigrants, and they tend to attack all immigrants altogether.

If you encounter those people in your daily life, understand they are at that stage, and they are just afraid and threatened. Don't try to explain or take it personally. It's a deeper issue for them, so walk away from them and be with people who accept you.

Ethnorelativism

Acceptance

In this first stage of ethnorelativism, people begin to recognize other cultures and accept them as viable alternatives to their worldview. They know that people are genuinely different from them and accept the inevitability of other value systems and behavioral norms. They do not yet adapt their behavior to the cultural context, but they no longer see other cultures as threatening, wrong, or inferior. People in the acceptance phase can be thought of as "culture-neutral," seeing differences as neither good nor bad but rather as a fact of life.

The example I gave you about the dream I had and the interpretation I held from my culture compared to the Chinese culture perfectly fits here. You accept others' worldviews or, in my case a dream, without making it wrong because it is different from your culture. This stage gives the window of opportunity to see the world; in other eyes. It will help you expand your perception of the world like you never have.

Adaptation

During the adaptation phase, people begin to view cultural differences as a valuable resource. Because differences are seen as positive, people consciously adapt their behaviors to the different cultural norms of their environment.

The example I gave you about the black color question I had fits well here. After I was free from the negative conception I had of Chinese people's characteristics, I transformed it into a positive one. I lived among the people appreciating their world, art, beautiful culture, and civilization. I enjoyed living in China while nurturing meaningful relationships with the locals. I even picked up some of their language that helped me survive there for two years.

Most people in the US belong to this stage. They accept immigrants; they see cultural differences as valuable resources. They try different cuisines from different cultures; they are genuinely curious when you tell them you are from another country. They want to know you and your cultural background because they value diversity.

Integration

Integration is the last stage in one's journey away from ethnocentrism. In this stage, people accept that their identity is not based on any single culture. Once integrated, people can effortlessly and even unconsciously shift between worldviews and cultural frames of reference. Though they maintain their own cultural identity, they naturally integrate aspects of other cultures into it.

Once you have progressed to an ethnorelativistic view of cultural differences, you will, in essence, be bi-cultural. You will revel in cultural differences and be able to effortlessly take on subtle characteristics of the local culture. Your intercultural sensitivity will also affect how others view and treat you.

When you get to this stage it depends on your willingness to learn, your level of curiosity, and the work you put in—but we are all capable of reaching this stage. Getting to this stage is a beautiful process if you know ahead of time you are moving through those stages. It can be painful if you have no idea what is happening to you, and it can be scary because you have no idea who you are becoming, and we try to avoid jumping from one stage to another because we fear we might lose who we are as we know it.

For me, the first three stages were excruciating, and maybe the adoption part sometimes was tough. However, I started to recognize what stage I was going through, the path I was taking, and my struggle stopped.

Being fully integrated doesn't require you to abandon your values or your community. Still, it requires you to be a powerful leader in your community because your worldview is broad, and you not only see from one angle but multiple angles.

You will also be a leader in the broader scale of the US culture. Your perspective, not seeing the US culture only from the US perspective, is a gift, and it will give you a lot of respect from others. You will be able to see problems from different angles, and people actually will value your opinions and your perspective.

It is the stage where you feel like you belong to this country, and it goes even further. At this point, you have a broader perspective under your belt, excitement, and full confidence that if you work hard, your American dream is yours to grasp, no matter what that might be.

Now you know these stages of integration, things become more evident. You no longer question what is happening to you. Still, you understand you are on the path to different stages in your integration and that what is happening to you in different stages is nothing but a process.

Once you understand that the pain of unlearning and undoing usually becomes less painful as you continue forward, you can now see a path and find yourself reaching success. When you meet negative people who tell you what to do to survive in America and complain, you now have a reference. You will understand what stage they are in, and you can better determine what advice to take from them and what you prefer to ignore.

Don't forget cultural integration works both ways. People who have lived in the US have to integrate into the overall, ever-evolving US culture with many immigrants living in it. Understanding this, instead of condemning and gossiping about them, trying to make them wrong for not understanding you, now you can be compassionate enough to see that they are just in a process like you. They may not be at the same stage, but remember that they are in the same process; everyone gets to integrate in their own time, and that's okay.

However, I have to warn you: Some people may be stuck in the first two stages for many years. Don't be discouraged; you don't know why they haven't moved to the next stage or why they're not fully integrated. All you can do is work on yourself and become fully integrated.

People feel inspired to do what they weren't able to do for many years by observing others. Don't tell people how they are wrong, how they are stuck, or how they should live their lives. Don't try to convince people; do your inner work and be fully integrated and live by example. You will be surprised to see people around you change their ways just by observing.

By now, I hope it is easy to see what stage you are in. You could be in between stages; it's okay, as long as you can see yourself where you are. You might even find yourself in different stages at different times. Sometimes I still vacillate from stage to stage. It's not a straight line.

As you go through this book, you will learn navigating tools to make your experience of going from one stage to another much easier, faster, and even enjoyable. I am so thrilled about your journey.

CHAPTER 2

THE TOP FOUR SURVIVOR NEEDS

When you move to a new place, your needs will be plentiful. Your new world has been spliced and mashed up with your former. What was simple and routine is nonexistent. Whether you moved to your new country for a new job, are an immigrant without a job, or refugee, you will have many survival needs.

It helps to move to your new country with a job in place or have close family, parents, or siblings who are established. Your family or friends can point you in the right direction immediately. Although you are not immune from the pain, it makes the transition more manageable with a support system already in place. However, if you are like most of us, it's not how it usually goes.

In most cases, you have to figure it out while going through integration, which takes a lot of your time, resources, and money. However, there are four top needs that are urgent right after you have moved to your new country.

Top Need #1: Communication

The most essential and crucial part of communication is transferring information from one place to another. Communication is a very complex topic since there is more than one way of communicating with one another.

The four primary communication modalities are:

- Verbal: Face-to-face, telephone, and other media
- Nonverbal: Gestures and body language in general
- Written: Books, magazines, letters, Internet social media
- Visualizations: Drawings, charts.

Professor Albert Mehrabian has pioneered the understanding of communications since the 1960s. According to Professor Mehrabian, communication is only seven percent verbal and ninety-three percent non-verbal. The non-verbal component consists of body language (fifty-five percent) and tone of voice (thirty-eight percent). You can find more information about Professor Albert Mehrabian's work and his research on his website: http://www.kaaj.com/psych/.

Of course, it doesn't mean your verbal communication isn't essential. It's vital to know how to communicate using any language. However, for our purposes, I would like to express that when you come to the US, you are not only learning the language but non-verbal communication too. It's challenging because the nonverbal communication you learned in your home country may be different. Some might even have the opposite meaning. You will have to learn nonverbal communication simultaneously while learning the English language. It is true when you move to any country and learn the language of that country.

In my third year studying at the University of Asmara, we had a course titled Cultural Anthropology. It was my favorite course ever. I remember our professor telling us that in some cultures, like in Tibet, sticking your tongue out when greeting someone is normal and acceptable, while in most countries, this is a form of insult. I remember my classmates and I were sticking our tongues out and seeing how it would feel while greeting someone. We did that for about a week, and we found it very amusing and surprised there could be such a difference in nonverbal communications in two different cultures.

So when you move to the US or any other country for that matter, don't rush in judging the culture before you learn the country's nonverbal communication. Learning nonverbal communication might take anywhere from a year to ten years, depending on how willing and open you are to learn. So be patient with yourself as you learn these new skills.

When you go to a new country, and if you are like me, you are traveling from a developing nation to a developed or western country, it could be overwhelming. Everything you see is magnified; it's noisy, loud, and fast-paced, especially if you moved to a large city like New York or San Francisco.

As I mentioned above, before coming to the USA, my very first experience in a large city was Beijing, China, in early 2004. I remember the mere sight of the city was frightening. I did not understand what I was feeling. The emotions and feelings I had were foreign to me. On the same day, I went from feeling so happy about seeing something new to feeling so fearful of what I didn't understand, feeling intimidated by someone or something, and sad for missing what was familiar. It wasn't easy sorting out all that I felt because I never felt all those feelings all at once. I had no idea how to understand and manage my feelings and emotions. The whole process was so complicated and confusing, especially before I could communicate a little bit better with the people around me.

People didn't speak English around me, including doctors and professors; their education mode was Chinese, so they all spoke Chinese, mandarin, to be specific. I had to have an interpreter go with me to important places, and that interpreter was as fascinated by me as I with her and her "crazy city."

Months later, I traveled all night by train to my final destination, which was Dalian, China. It was a smaller city and less crazy than Beijing, but still more prominent than the African city I had left behind. Dalian was always loud for me, the weather was too cold, and I had never seen snow before moving to Dalian.

The language sounded so irritating to me and even funny because I didn't understand it, and I was frustrated. The city had its scent that was not familiar to me. I felt so small in Dalian, where I didn't know the language nor the culture. And more importantly, I didn't understand my reaction because it was all new to me. I remember having nightmares, not sleeping because of loud traffic, and feeling so sensitive, fearful, angry, anxious, and depressed.

I've always been independent, even as a kid, so I was not fond of the limitations imposed on me. Therefore, I did what came naturally to me; I started using body language to communicate, studying language, and learning keywords like, "I am sorry I don't speak the language," "What does that mean?" "How are you?" "I am new here," and most importantly, "Please don't put MSG in my food." As I found out, I was allergic to monosodium glutamate (MSG), a flavor enhancer commonly added to Chinese food.

Once I started communicating, my level of frustration went down. Communication is so important, I can't stress this enough. Communication is everything! Fast forward to now: I see my almost-three-year-old son feeling irritated, frustrated, throwing a tantrum, and crying because he wants something or wants to do something, but he doesn't know how to communicate his needs yet fully. The crying and annoyance subside when he can point to what he wants and somehow communicate his needs through words.

Your frustration, anger, crying, and all negative feelings you may feel when you move to a new place are normal. Yep, you heard me; it is all normal. And like kids, we might shout at people or even throw an adult temper tantrum. Some people may expect you to be and act like an adult without knowing your background. If your behavior is different than expected, it can be perceived as a mental illness.

Don't worry, I understand; I've been there! Please don't believe it for one minute when others tell you that you are not normal. You are 100% normal, and you may be experiencing some troubling circumstances, and you are doing everything you can to adjust and survive. In some cases, you might have trauma from war or other horrible events that happened to you, and since that trauma is still there not yet healed, you might magnify the negative emotions you feel. In that case, you need help to heal the trauma by talking to a therapist. I have worked with psychologists and have seen them help trauma patients to recover. If you fall into this category, what you feel is normal, you need to heal from it.

You may need to seek services for mental health. It will be to your advantage because you will have to learn new skills to replace the behavior that doesn't serve you, gets you into trouble with others, or even puts you in danger. You will learn how to change your behavior, accept new norms and values of the new culture, and how to effectively express yourself. It will be helpful to understand what is culturally appropriate. What you're going through is a normal reaction to the changes that may be happening around you. So buckle up; I never said it was easy! But you can make learning new things fun and adventurous. Why not? It's better than learning while feeling miserable. Learn the English language, and simultaneously the nonverbal communication.

Strategies to Learn English

- Enroll in an English language class and promise yourself that you will not deviate from continuing until there is no need for you to go there anymore. And ask your teacher about the meaning of any nonverbal communication you observed in your daily life.

- Find online resources, buy books or audiobooks that you can listen to on your phone or CD player wherever you go.
- Don't be shy.
- Practice makes perfect, so practice with every opportunity you find. I meet many people through my job who understand English correctly, but when it comes to speaking it, they feel lost due to a lack of practice using English.

  Tell the people you are interacting with that you are learning English and to forgive you in advance if you make mistakes. This will allow the other person to be more patient in communicating with you. It will also enable the other person to practice empathy, and he/she might correct you gently when you make mistakes.

- Always be proud of yourself for learning something new and appreciate yourself and your efforts, which will give you a boost to go for more things to learn.
- Tell people when you are feeling sad, frustrated, and depressed. Let them know that you are new in this country and learning so much rapidly that it is taking a toll on you. Most people will understand your situation better than you expect once they know the context. What they will not understand is an outburst of those feelings without a context. So be honest.
- There is a saying: Rome wasn't built in a day. And learning to speak like the natives will take time. Be patient with yourself and reward yourself for where you are. Some people live their

whole life without ever learning a second language, so you are doing something that some people don't get to do. In general, people who can speak more than one language tend to be considered intelligent and admired. So own it!

- Challenge yourself. Just getting by with what you have isn't enough. If you are on level one, challenge yourself to level two; if you are on level two, challenge yourself to level three.

I am currently studying Italian, so I can communicate with my in-laws who live in Italy. Currently, I am at level one, and I am pushing myself to level two. There is a sense of confidence that comes when you challenge yourself to accomplish something, even if you haven't reached your goal yet. You are on your way.

In the next chapter, we will go in-depth about communication, but for now, if you are a newbie, this information is enough to get you by.

Top Need #2: A Place to Live

If you moved because there was a job waiting for you in your new country, moved to a country where they provide housing and money for a while, or you already have family members in your new country and are reunited with them, then great! Good for you! You may skip this part. For the rest of us, the biggest challenge in coming to a new country is finding a place to live independently.

Like I mentioned before, when I first came to the US, my relatives picked me up from the airport, and I went straight to their home. I had a separate bedroom waiting for me. I was fortunate. However, it was a couple of months before finding my place and declaring my independence. This process isn't easy, especially in larger cities of the US.

Learning about everyone's shared problems in your new country will give you some relief. What is happening to you is also happening to everyone else, even people who were born and grew up in the state. Know that you are not alone in this process. It helps that you do not fall to a victim mentality and waste your time thinking why this is happening to you. It's not happening only to you. It is happening to people everywhere. You have walked into an existing social problem. It isn't personal.

Housing is a huge economic problem in most major cities for most people. If you live in California, Google "housing," and what you will see will surprise you: You will learn that housing is a massive problem in this state.

If you live outside of California, explore what the housing situation is in your area. Now that we have the technology, information is at the tips of our fingers. Use it. If you are not good at surfing the internet because you came from a country where the internet was found only in cafes, go to your local public library and ask someone to help you find out about housing.

Your local library is an excellent resource for you. In most cities, they are free and have books and computers you can use for at least an hour at a time. And, if you have a laptop, you can get Wi-Fi and do your research. So pack your lunch and probably dinner too, and camp out there, researching, and studying. While writing parts of this book, I was at my local library. It offers all kinds of free stuff, the information is quick to find, and they also have programs for kids. I use the library frequently.

If you have a social worker, write down all the questions for the next time you see her/him. Let them help you find the resources you might need. Working with your social worker is useful, and it saves you time to do other things on your long to-do list. Use their knowledge and expertise as a resource.

Do your research! Your first step is research about the situation of housing in your area. Either on the internet, your community, or ask people around you. People love to tell you what they know.

If you live in a refugee camp and are waiting in another country to immigrate to the US or any other country, or just considering and planning on moving, having internet access will help to do this research before you even arrive. I regret not doing more research because my focus on the logistics of how to get here.

If you move to an expensive place, like California, consider these options:

- If you are staying with your relatives and getting along with them, stay with them till you have other options available to you.

- Find a roommate. People you already know would be an ideal option for you since you already know the person. If you don't find someone you know who is looking for a roommate, then check out your local newspaper, use the internet, and websites like craigslist www.craigslist.org. Practice caution and always be careful meeting people on the internet. Don't forget that there are many good people in the world. There are also bad people looking to take advantage of you. Ask around, word of mouth is an excellent way to find roommates. Chances are, there are so many people around you that are looking for a roommate like you.

I know this is hard for most people, but if you can, be open-minded in finding people different than you. Choosing roommates from a different culture than yours is a wonderful opportunity for you to expand your perspective on other cultures and practice your English.

- Research live-in/work arrangements. If you don't mind working with elderly or if you love kids, many people hire caregivers or nannies to live with them and take care of their kids or elders. With this kind of arrangement, you get both a job and a place to stay. It's perfect!

- In extreme circumstances, check with your local shelters to see if you can stay there until your circumstances change. Some shelters will only allow you to sleep there at night and might not allow you to stay during the day. I remember meeting someone who told me that he was living in shelters for a few months and was spending his days at the library, filling out applications for jobs, and looking for housing. It took time, but he was able to find a decent job, found roommates that he got along with, and after a few years, enrolled himself in a school to get his social work bachelor's degree and got a better job helping people with their problems. He eventually got married, bought a home, and lives happily. It's a happy ending story. I admire and respect this person for his bravery and hard work in making his American dream happen. It doesn't matter where you start, but it matters where you end up, no matter how long it takes you to get there.

- Move to areas you can afford. If the housing you are looking for is too expensive, look in your city for areas where the rent might be affordable and move there temporarily until you can afford something better.

In America, when young people turn 18, they are considered adults, and some are ready to move out of their parent's homes. Parents would like their children to be independent and go out in the world on their own. Young adults face many difficulties when it comes to housing, jobs, and figuring out their lives in this big adult world with so little at hand unless they have wealthy parents or parents who make many sacrifices to help their young adult children along the way of life.

These days, the cost of living is so high that many young adults choose to stay with their parents until they save up for a place of their own. Most parents are adjusting and support their kids in achieving their goals to become responsible and independent adults.

However, young adults with limited resources have to do what we immigrants do when we come to America. Go out there, find a place to live, a job, and a support system. And their struggle is like ours; although they might have the advantage of the language, they still face a lot of hardship.

Avoid having a victim mentality. Victim mentality makes you see everything as if it happened only to you. Find out the facts, and what's a struggle for everyone around you. That way, your focus will shift to the solution instead of being stuck in feeling sorry for yourself. Your mind will look for what others use for solutions. If you don't understand what the greater community deals with, you will spend years feeling victimized, and when we are in a victim mentality, we can't use our minds to find solutions to our problems.

For most new immigrants that I work with, as it was for me, it's hard to imagine that Americans are going through the same issues and problems that we go through. We think it's only our problem. I always bring to my client's attention the bigger picture at hand. I tell them stories of what some of my American friends deal with and go through, with the consent given by my friends, of course.

I see the shocked looks on their faces saying, "What? But they were born here." And I tell them, "Yeah, but this problem you are facing isn't only because you moved here, it is a social problem in this area." Shifting your mind to that idea gives you access to solutions faster.

Once your mind focuses on solutions, list the different solutions available to you. Whether you will stay with relatives or friends for free while saving up for a place or find your roommates, decide what you want and put all your energy and time into moving towards the solution you have found. Always know that what you choose is a "for now" solution, and you don't have to live that way forever.

Being indecisive about something makes us prone to being overwhelmed and can rob us of our energy and cause us stress. So whatever it is, please do your research, be honest about what would work for you or what you can do at the time, and decide to move towards it. Easy, right?

Top Need # 3: A Support System

A support system is defined as a group of people who give someone help, money, encouragement, etc. Another definition: Facilities and people who interact and remain in informal communication for mutual assistance: a network that enables you to live in a certain style. We will discuss support systems in more detail later in this chapter; however, for now, if you are new in the US, it is important to understand the importance of a support system.

Humans are social animals; whether we like it or not, we have been surrounded by people since we were born. It doesn't matter if you were born at the hospital or home; no matter how you arrived in this world, you were at least with your mother; if not, perhaps many other people were waiting for your arrival, welcoming you.

The same thing happens when we die, we will have people we don't even know come to our funeral to pay their respect.

As we go through life, while we are on this earth, our ride will be experiencing ups and downs. We need others to travel this journey called life with us. We want people who understand us and who we can depend on during tough times. We need people who will listen to us and give us honest feedback. We need people who will love us, and we can love in return. We need people with who we can share our happiness with.

> *Research has proven that having a support system has many positive benefits, such as higher levels of well-being, better coping skills, and longer and healthier life. Studies have also shown that social support can reduce depression and anxiety. Some people do best with a large support group, while others need a small support system. Giving and receiving support from others is a basic human need.*
>
> *(By Cathy Williams, MSW, LCSW, CEAP)*
> *https://www.bjceap.com/Blog/ArtMID/448/ArticleID*
> */139/TheImportance-of-Developing-a-Support-System*

When it comes to immigrants, it is a very vital and essential piece of cultural integration. Sometimes, I meet newly arrived immigrants through my work, and when coaching them, they say to me that they don't understand why they are feeling sad, lonely, or excessively emotional. When I ask if there are people around they can talk to, their answer is usually "no," and they tell me that all of their family and friends are in the country they left behind. I encourage them to think of where they can find people they might relate to, such as a church, mosque, or community center, and I suggest going somewhere where it is comfortable to meet and connect with people. Because without a support system in place, it's challenging to adapt to your environment as new arrivals. So if you have a church, mosque, or community center in your area, start there. Find people to support you emotionally and mentally.

Therapist/Counselor

After finding people they can talk to in their community, some people still feel anxious and depressed. When this happens, they get confused and can't figure out what is wrong with them.

Don't be afraid to look for a therapist or a counselor. Finding the right therapist or counselor could be your most effective support system if you like and trust them. I know, I know, for most people this could be scary, and when I suggest this kind of support system, people mostly say, "But I am not crazy! I am fine; I don't need that." I understand!

Going through the same thing myself after first living in Ethiopia, then Eritrea, China, and the US—all totally different cultures—I am blessed to shine a light on this because I went through the same confusion, to the point of being misdiagnosed with bipolar disorder. I hope my sharing this experience may reach someone in this space as they're reading this book.

As much as I love the US, more than I could have imagined, and all the technology, education, and expertise, it is not absolute. There is no perfection in this world. Start questioning everything that your good judgment tells you to. Get it in your head that everything you hear isn't necessarily the truth.

The first time I went to a mental health professional was in China. The whole idea was new to me. I was taught in my culture that going to a therapist means being crazy. The very idea of seeing a therapist was scary, and I didn't understand why I was there.

However, one tool that helped me was being honest with my therapist. I told him exactly how I felt about being in therapy. My honesty allowed him to educate me about mental health. He forever altered my life not only by educating me about the field but giving me the tools I needed to navigate my feelings and emotions, manage them, and identify them.

Before meeting my therapist, I had no idea my thoughts were separate from my feelings and emotions, and what was weird to me was what he told me in our first session, that I could manage and control my feelings and emotions. Wow! It didn't make sense to me. It would take me another eight years to fully understand and put it into practice. I made it a constant practice in my life.

When I came to the US, my world was shattered again. I was desperate to understand everything because it was a matter of survival for me. I had to work harder than anyone else I knew because I was a single mom. I also felt that I had to work three times as hard because I was the mother of a special needs child. Not understanding the system—and how to get what I needed and wanted for my and me, or how to discover what was available: where to get it, what is and is not appropriate—was making it challenging.

My lack of security and stability in my life brought a lot of pain, stress, frustration, and, most of all, anxiety. I have had a few panic attacks, and I had never heard about anxiety or panic attacks before, let alone experienced them. You can imagine my terror of what I didn't know.

I decided to seek mental health counseling, and I found one that I felt comfortable with. After seeing me for two days, she misdiagnosed me as bipolar. That was the first time I heard of the diagnosis. I asked the therapist what "bipolar" meant, and she gave me some resources and told me not to worry about anything. She told me that I could collect social security disability and get money and live comfortably collecting a monthly disability check. What she didn't understand was that living on social security disability would have been a death sentence for me. I didn't come to the US to get a social security check and get comfortable. I came here for a better life for my son and myself; I was here for an American dream. As you can imagine, I was devastated with the diagnosis the therapist had suggested. I went home and did a lot of research while taking the prescribed medicine, which didn't help because I was feeling worse. I was constantly lethargic and borderline depressed. I had yet to learn about all this medical terminology.

The more I read, the more confused I was about this diagnosis, so I told my therapist on my next visit that I didn't think I had bipolar disorder and that my body was rejecting the medicine she had prescribed. She said, "We need to change the medication because usually it takes time to find the right medicine that your body will like." I tried three different medications while doing more research on the diagnosis, and my body still rejected the medication, to the point of not being able to function. From what I read, I was more and more convinced that I wasn't bipolar. I wanted to quit taking the medicine and was tempted never to go back to the therapist.

But I knew, from what I read, that stopping the medication was dangerous. Going off medication without a doctor's approval may have more complications than benefits. I revisited my therapist; I was terrified, and I felt that what I wanted to say to her might have been offensive. To my surprise, she told me that I had a right to refuse treatment or to change therapists or doctors. She also reminded me that she told me about my rights in the beginning. I had probably heard them and didn't understand what they meant.

I was happy she wasn't upset. I gathered my courage and told her that, based on research I didn't believe her diagnosis was accurate. I admitted that something was happening to me, but bipolar was not it. The fact that my body was rejecting the medicine was enough of a sign for me. I told her I would trust my body and to please help me get off the medicine; and I promised her I would get a second opinion from another therapist because I valued my life and my mental health.

She agreed; I slowly stopped the medication I was talking with her guidance. Since I was committed to my life and my mental health, I did see one more therapist. Finally, I got a diagnosis that felt right.

Anxiety due to cultural adjustment issues. The second doctor told me that the symptoms likely gave my first therapist the idea of a bipolar diagnosis. But this doctor was familiar with the symptoms of cultural adjustment anxiety because he was an immigrant who experienced these himself when he came to the US a long time ago. With everything this doctor was explaining to me, I felt seen and understood.

I am sharing this story because I have met many immigrants in the US telling me similar therapist stories, and they disagreed with their diagnosis. They stop taking the prescribed medicine, don't return to therapy, and struggle in their lives. Please don't do that. Your mental health is too important to risk something like that. If you don't agree with your therapist or don't like them, you have a right to switch to someone you feel more comfortable with. Politely ask the therapist to help you transition to another therapist of your choosing.

After the right diagnosis, I understood that I had always been anxious, which affected my mental health tremendously. I was not eating right, staying up late trying to read, research, think, and plan my life, which provoked strange behavior during the day. I experienced a lack of sleep and excess worry about the future. The doctor prescribed an anti-anxiety medication to take as needed when I felt overwhelmed and couldn't sleep. He helped me find the right social worker/therapist who worked with me for almost two years.

Ms. Clara, the social worker/therapist, addressed everything I was dealing with daily and taught me the tools I could use to overcome difficulties. My therapist was indeed my heaven-sent angel disguised in a social worker mask.

Slowly but surely, I found myself dealing with my emotions better. I continued to take anti-anxiety medication as needed until my therapist and I decided I didn't need it any longer. I graduated from my therapy and stopped going after two years because my social worker felt that I had all the tools I needed to deal with my emotions all on my own. When I slept better, ate right, managed my worries, and learned some positive behavior, I was ready to conquer the world.

You might be going through something similar to what I was and if you are, I can tell you, there is nothing wrong with seeking mental help. In fact, it's very smart to seek mental health counseling while going through your cultural integration process.

Although I no longer see a therapist, therapy was one of my strong support systems, helping me go through tough times and identify what I was feeling. It taught me a lot about setting boundaries, loving myself, building healthy relationships, how to build trust, and a lot more.

In the US, where family values are fading away and more people are avoiding churches, therapists and counselors are an excellent support system while you are getting used to and adapting to the US culture. You may see your therapists for one year, two, or ten years; it doesn't matter how long, as long as you are finding value and reliable support to help you go through it all. Check your health insurance to find a therapist in your network. However, be selective about who you choose as your therapist. In most western countries (check if this is true for your country if you are reading this from another country), you have the right to change your doctor, your therapist, or your caseworker if you feel like they are not right for you. Just be polite about it.

You can also ask for someone you will be more comfortable with. If you feel more comfortable with women, choose a woman, and communicate your preference. Forget about hurting their feelings;

they are professionals and can handle it when you tell them you want someone else. They are there to help you.

If you feel comfortable with someone who speaks your language, communicate that without being afraid or shy. I know it sounds weird for some people who come from a country where this idea is foreign, and I am counting myself in that, but you can get used to choosing what is comfortable for you. You could also select someone from your religion if that is important to you.

Choose someone you like, who you think will make you feel comfortable and safe to open up to. That is the key. You can be free to open up about your life and tell the therapist everything that is going on with you as if they are your best friend!

I know this is true in the US. What you say in your therapy sessions stays there. However, please check with your therapist if what you say in therapy is kept confidential so that you can feel safe enough to talk. It is your right to advocate for your needs and get the help you need.

Another way for you to expand your support system is to make new friends in your new country.

Make New Friends

If you came with your family, your family and relatives are sound emotional support systems. You can share with them your worries, your fears, frustrations, hopes, and dreams.

If you are in your new country by yourself, then you can look for your community. Just make sure your community isn't divided by politics and ideologies or religion that make you feel lost in their agenda. It is a huge issue for a lot of immigrants I coach.

Whenever you visit a community center, see how you feel. Some questions to ask yourself are:

- Do I feel comfortable? Do I feel safe?
- Can I express myself fully without being afraid?
- Am I getting value from being here?
- Can I grow personally while contributing here?
- Do I feel supported?

If you answer yes to all the above, congratulations, you have found one of your support systems. And guess what? By doing so, you just have become someone's support in the process.

If you are religious, find out if there is a spiritual gathering for your religion. Most people choose to go to the churches, mosques, or spiritual gatherings who speak their language, and that is good.

If you feel courageous enough, and you would like to expand your learning, find the spiritual group of your choice, which speaks the language of English or your new country. The advantage here will be that you have found a support system, but you can improve your language. Yes, you've hit two birds with one stone. Another contribution you would make that isn't even on your radar yet is to help those from a different background in that church or community center. How, you ask? You would be helping them understand your culture, which contributes to the larger community's cultural integration. And who knows, one of the people there might have a company and looking to hire a new employee, and may have always been curious but unsure about hiring immigrants, and just knowing you might help someone else get hired. Because of you, this person might feel comfortable hiring someone from your culture. It might even be you! It's a smart move!

Another support system is for you to make new friends who have similar interests and ideas as you. A lot of my clients and people I meet ask, "How can I make friends now? I am too old to make new friends. I wouldn't even know how it's possible to make friends at this age?" I understand the feeling, and I can empathize with it. Thanks to technology, we can now keep in touch with our friends from high school, college, and back home. However, it's equally important to find new friends in your new country because these new friends will understand what challenges, dreams, and hopes you face currently. You can create a strong support system that can nurture you and find a place to turn to. The bigger your challenges, the bigger the support group you need. I have an extensive support system around me, which is why I can do what I'm able to do.

People often ask me, "How do you do it? You have a challenging life, and yet you always seem joyful, loving, and it looks like you are enjoying your life." I tell them one of my secrets: I keep my extensive support system around me. I have my family for emotional support, my women's circle for spiritual and soul support, a writer's meetup group and association for my writing needs, and exercise buddies for my exercise goal support. I have different self-development organizations that I belong to, and they always keep me on my toes for self development. I have my old friends that I keep around who know me in good times and bad times. They keep me laughing, advise me, remind me of who I am when I forget. I have a wonderful nurse who takes good care of my child with special needs at home and supports me in making my life possible. Oh yeah, the support system equals happiness. Let me say that, again, a healthy and robust support system equals happiness.

You will have to, of course, learn to get along with people (if that's an issue), gain tools on managing and nurturing all the support systems around you, and give time to it all, but you can accomplish the goal. You might not need an extensive support system as I do; however, you will still need a support system that works for you.

If you want great friends, be a great friend yourself. You also need to be a good friend material yourself. You must be dependable and trustworthy and do self-development if you don't know how to be that person. Friendship is a two-way lane. You need to be the person you want others to be before looking for one.

No one expects anyone to be perfect; however, you need to be kind, sensitive to others' feelings, have open communication with your friends, and consistently learn how to be better for yourself and others.

In his book, **7 Habits of Highly Effective People**, Stephen Covey says that it's critical: *Seek first to understand, then to be understood*, which is true. To understand others, we need to brush up on our communication skills, and develop our listening skills like a muscle.

Start listening to others, try to understand them, try to put yourself in their situation, and see if you can understand their world and perception.

Start communicating with your family and friends also, talking about your feelings and sharing your ideas and stories about your culture with whoever you meet. No one wants to be friends with a robot. If you can't open up about how you are feeling and about the different things you are experiencing, you might have shallow friendships that can't be considered true support groups.

I know it is hard to be open about feelings if you are not used to it, incredibly hard. Start by talking about how you feel about that movie you just saw the other day with someone who has watched it. Talk about how it made you feel. Ask them also what they thought about the film. It is a perfect way to find out about someone's values, thoughts about things, and their belief system; as you share yours. It will help deepen your friendships when you're comfortable. You could start by talking about your feelings, your day, the crazy man you saw who was rude to you. If you have kids, what about their behavior this morning? The weather, and how different it is from your home country or places you have visited. Sharing our feelings and emotions about things creates a connection. Learn to trust and share more private things about your life even when you don't feel comfortable.

However, proceed with caution. Don't just talk to a new friend about your family secrets. Only share your important secrets to a friend who has proven worthy of receiving you and caring for your secret. Please share with friends who will keep what you tell them to themselves, not use what you tell them against you, but give you sound advice. A real friend cares for you no matter what, and they will have proven that they can be trusted over and over again.

Early in my exploring friendships, I made mistakes, as many people do. I would make a friend, and sometimes with certain friendships, I experienced an instantly strong connection. Without any precautions, I felt that I could share things that were very personal that I didn't usually share with others. Sadly, I soon found that my secrets or confidential information shared with others was not for their ears. Other friends I connected with this way saw that I had no boundaries and withdrew from me.

After dealing with such incidents for many years, I thought that people couldn't be trusted, that there were no real friends, and that making friends was hard. I also had heard these comments and feelings from others. However, now that I am wiser because of experience, I know that it was my fault! I didn't know any better at the time, but it was my responsibility. I learned that great connections don't always equal trust. Trust is earned, not felt. It was a massive lesson for me throughout my twenties and part of my thirties.

Be careful not to be open about your secrets initially with new friends. However, don't be frightened to make new connections. Just have some boundaries. The trust will come later while you are building your friendships. You will know who you can tell personal information to and who will only hear your simple matters. You will recognize the friends you can completely trust with your life secrets as well. Not all friendships are equal. Understanding this will help you build your best friendships. More on this later.

And who knows, you may even find your significant other while building friendships. By the way, if you are looking for your significant other, you might want to consider online dating. Initially, the idea of online dating was so irritating and embarrassing to me, and later, that is how I met some of the good friends I have, and believe it or not, my husband as well. So be open and brave. Being open-minded while still respecting your values serves you well in your new country.

Top Need #4: Finding a Job

Finding a job to support yourself and your family in a place with a higher cost of living than your country of origin is one of your most urgent needs.

I live in one of the most expensive regions in the US. Finding a job, paying bills and expenses, worrying about finances, paying rent or the mortgage, and saving for retirement is a worry that all Californians share, immigrants and nonimmigrants alike. So if you live in a big city like San Francisco, New York, and others, it's a common issue that you have walked into.

When I first moved to the US, I thought everyone was rich. It seemed everyone had their lives figured out, looked polished, and although I didn't know car models, I knew by instinct that they drove nice, expensive cars. The people I saw were rich enough to afford to send their kids to daycare, go on vacations, and didn't have much to worry about. I believed this was heaven, and I wanted to be part of it.

Later, I slowly discovered that all I thought was not true: Worries we immigrants have are common to most people in America as well. Based on a survey, only 3.5 percent of the 100 million households in America are considered wealthy. So, don't feel isolated and lose confidence in your interaction with others. You have more things in common than you could imagine.

Yes, you are new here, and that means you have to start from scratch. You might feel depressed. After all, you now might have to do jobs beneath your qualifications and education because you need to survive.

You didn't think this was how things would turn out. But it is. Accept it and know this is only temporary. Be grateful to get jobs that you can gain experience in, if not in what you actually do, then at least in interacting with colleagues, American bosses, and the work system.

When I arrived in the US, I had a bachelor's degree and experience working with nonprofits and the United Nations. I thought I was going to start a job the day after I arrived in the US. I confidently made plans to bring my son to the US within six months. I assumed that my education and work experience would qualify me to start the right job. Instead, I crashed to the ground. I slammed so hard that even my bones felt like they had cracked for real. At some point, I didn't feel like getting out of bed in the morning; I thought I had made a big mistake coming to the US, and I had failed my son and my future.

I was shocked when my best friend Simret, who came to the US six months prior, gently explained that I might not be able to get the job I thought I could get. I should apply for other types of jobs like cleaning or caregiving while still not giving up on my hope for jobs that fit my educational background and qualifications.

The disappointment, the horror, and the sadness I felt was so tremendous that it had a massive mental health impact on me. I thought I was coming for a better life, and I was facing shock because I couldn't have my dream job right away. Instead, I was going to do jobs I wouldn't even do in the country I left.

So, I had to stay focused in the face of a temporary setback. I had to get my son to the US within six months because if I didn't, my son would lose his visa and green card privileges, and he would have had to wait five years, until I had become an American citizen, to join me in the US.

Some people advised me that I would have to wait five years to bring my son to the US, after getting well established. They informed me that I could focus on becoming a US citizen, getting my dream job, and having a home I could call my own before I call for my son.

However, this idea was unacceptable to me. I felt perhaps this idea may have worked for others, but not for me. My purpose in coming to the US was to give my special needs son a life that he couldn't have back home. If I couldn't bring him to be with me in six months, I would instead go back home. I needed to be by his side, helping him with his life challenges.

My only choice was to work extremely hard and bring my son to the US in six months. I wasn't willing to live in the US without my son, knowing that he not only would grow up without services he urgently needed for his survival, but he would grow up without his mom. I wasn't willing to accept that option. So, I was shocked, but I was willing to do any kind of job.

Two months after I arrived, I got a job as a caregiver. It was the only thing that appealed to me since I am a nurturing person and had experience taking care of elderly extended family and my special needs child when I was back home. But I never thought I would make a career out of it.

In the US, agencies control the job market. They get a percentage of your earned money, up to 50% in some instances for connecting you with clients. The agency I applied to accepted me, gave me an orientation, and assigned me to a sweet older woman I immediately adored and, later, her family.

Usually, the agency sends caregivers to different locations on different days; however, after my first week, the agency asked if I would consider being a live-in caregiver for the lady I was assigned. The assignment was to live and work four days a week, and I could live there the rest of the week. It sounded like a great deal to me and my ticket to freedom from my current living situation. I accepted it. I worked diligently, saving every penny I made for the arrival of my son. With generous support from friends and my employer, I was able to bring my dad and my son right before my son's visa expiration deadline. It took another four years to land my dream job which I love and enjoy at the moment.

Don't lose heart if you come to the US with a doctorate or an engineering degree, if you had a respectable lifestyle back home, and all of a sudden it's gone, and you feel the choices available are beneath you. Maybe the job available to you is working as a cashier, cleaning, caregiver, or an Uber or Lyft driver. I suggest that you accept it, and don't disrespect any job. Please trust me; you will learn a lot about yourself and the people around you. There is not one job I worked that I regret in my life. Don't get me wrong. I've had jobs where I didn't like the boss, I didn't like the people I worked with, and didn't like the pay. However, those jobs gave me experience in dealing with others, in managing my time, and in so many more ways than I can't list here. Take the job. With hard work, persistence, dedication, and not losing sight of who you are and what you are meant to do, along with taking small steps towards your goals, you can definitely make it. Don't be ashamed you had to work jobs which you believe are beneath you, instead be proud that you were willing to be flexible.

One amazing resource I want to offer you is a nonprofit, Upwardly Global (https://www.upwardlyglobal.org). They will guide you on finding a job similar to what you did before moving to the USA. It took me three years to find them, and once I did, they helped me tremendously in crafting my resume. Check to see if you qualify for their program. They have both physical and virtual offices in many states.

Find community resources available to you. Search for vacancies on the internet, always look around you; most places advertise a job opening, or they might use the "help wanted" sign on their doors. Don't forget you are brave to come to a new country. Be brave again and go inside and ask them.

Be open-minded, take jobs that you usually wouldn't take. Lower your pride because this situation doesn't have to be forever and get to work and financially support yourself and your family. And be careful not to fall into a victim mentality where you think that is the only job you can do and you are stuck forever with that, and that is your fate in America.

This belief is typical, and it will come to your mind but let it go quickly whenever it comes to your mind because it's not true: you have to consider the situation as temporary unless you make it permanent by thinking this is all you can get.

You might see people from your community who have been in the US for ten, twenty years and maybe more doing the jobs they were doing when their first arrived, and they hate it. They are stuck in their mentality; when you talk to them, they are so negative, and they would tell you that is life in America. I have met many of them. By all means, avoid those people. Because their belief is wrong, and if you listen and follow them, you will end up in the same place.

They are stuck in their mentality; when you talk to them, they are so negative, and they would tell you that is life in America. I have met many of them. By all means, avoid those people. Because their belief is wrong, and if you listen and follow them, you will end up in the same place.

We will talk more about what kind of people to avoid and who to surround yourself with later in this book. At the same time you're doing the job to support your family, schedule a few hours a week to work on your dream job.

If you have to get a college degree to get your dream job, start taking one class per semester. If you must study for the bar exam, give yourself time to learn, schedule a few hours a week towards that goal, and use all the time you can for your future dream work.

Talk to people who are doing the job you would love to do. Ask them what steps you need to take to get the job. Work on the steps they share with you, and do your best. Slowly but surely, you will accomplish your dream job. Most of all, be grateful for the job you currently have and learn from the people involved in the job, your boss, and your colleagues. Make it a habit of being on time. Learn how to communicate with everyone around you. Perfect your language skills, and learn how to build your confidence. You can improve yourself in a job you might not even like. There is always an opportunity for growth, which will help you when you are ready for your next job.

I am sharing a fantastic story of a couple that I respect and admire. Sam and Elizabeth, husband and wife, came to the US four years before I arrived. Sam had a bachelor's degree and his wife was a high school graduate. Sam and Elizabeth had five children, including one set of twins. While trying to get settled in the US, they used every government resource to provide for their family. Sam got a job as a security guard, while Elizabeth worked at home caring for the two younger children. While still working as a security guard, Sam enrolled in a master's degree program for bio-health technology. He was determined to finish the program within five to seven years. Sam set aside time to study, even as he continued to help out with the older children's homework and other needs, and get rest. When the twins were five and enrolled in public school, Elizabeth found a part-time job as a caregiver and enrolled in a certified nursing assistant (CNA) course.

When Sam and Elizabeth were both working, they were less dependent on government assistance. However, they still needed help with food stamps and cash aid for their rent. Elizabeth received a raise and started attending a nearby college to achieve her new goal of becoming a licensed vocational nurse (LVN). It took her approximately two years to complete and receive her license while studying and working part time. After becoming an LVN, Elizabeth took a job with an agency that offered flexible hours so she could continue taking care of her family responsibilities.

Sam completed his master's program in four years instead of five and was hired by a reputable bio-health company in the Bay Area. The family was completely free of government assistance, and they were so proud of their achievements. After being in the US for fifteen years, I received an invitation from Elizabeth to celebrate her graduation when she became a Registered nurse (RN). I was so happy for them.

When I asked Elizabeth what her motivation was, she said, "I wanted to teach my children that they can be whoever they want to be in America if they work hard. I wanted to be an example to show them what you can achieve, not just tell them. I didn't want my children to grow up thinking they had to be dependent on a government assistance program. I wanted to teach them the importance of being self-reliant." Isn't that amazing? Sam said, "Now we plan to buy a house and save up more money for our children's college education. We're not done yet. We came for the American dream, and this is only the beginning."

I love this family so much because it is a perfect example of knowing who you are, being focused, and achieving your dreams while using all the resources around you to provide for you and your family.

Sam and Elizabeth could have said, "You know what, we have five children, we need to raise them, and we can probably achieve our dreams when they are eighteen. No, they were working hard and smart, fulfilling their dreams, and liberating themselves from government assistance. Being examples to their children is what was the motivation to be a hardworking family who doesn't give up on their dreams, but achieves them.

When I asked Same and Elizabeth what advice can they give to new immigrants, they said, "Not giving up is the key and to get to work and work hard." Elizabeth said smiling, "we need to remember, we didn't come to the US to settle and become dependent on assistance from the government. We came to thrive." I agree 100%.

Below I'm sharing about two other people; you can choose not to follow their examples. Remember, in America; you can be whoever you chose.

I met Alice, who's from Pakistan, through a friend. She had a master's degree, and when she first came to the US and realized the only place she was able to find work was a grocery store, she was devastated and embarrassed. Alice allowed her ego to get in her way, and she didn't care that others like her had to do similar jobs, not in the fields of their education, while they were building their future. She started avoiding the people trying to help her and cut ties with the excellent support she had. Alice fought with everyone and moved to another state where none of her friends and relatives could see what she was doing. Alice had become a bitter person who was jealous of other people achieving their dreams. She often responded with negative comments when someone would tell her positive news about their lives, like getting their dream job, getting married, or having children. She would try to make others feel inadequate for achieving something they worked hard to achieve. Eventually, people started to avoid her.

I saw Alice ten years ago, and it was sad to know that she was even more committed to her anger. She focused on how things "should be" instead of seeing her current situation as an opportunity to grow to the next level; in the end, how you want to spend your time is totally up to you.

Here is another example: I met Farhad, who is Iranian, about six years ago through a referral to help him because he was still having a hard time adjusting after being in the US for seven years.

At that time, I had lived in the US for about five years, and I had just started to get the hang of the US culture. Farhad told me that he had a good life in Iran, had a maid, lived like a "prince," and never had to worry about money. Farhad said that he had to find a lower-level job since moving to the US, and he was always depressed. He would get a job and get fired quickly, or he would quit because he didn't like this or that. Farhad was having a tough time adjusting to life in the US and letting go of the comfort he had left behind. To top this off, he was feeling lonely. He felt that most of the people in his community avoided him. Farhad wanted a wife to help him with his English because he had an idea for a business, and his English was limited. I asked Farhad why he didn't enroll in adult school to learn English. He gave me a bunch of excuses like, "I don't have time," "I can't understand what the teacher says," and "It's hard to learn when you are older." I honestly tried to help Farhad. I suggested a lot of things he could do to improve his language. For about a month, all I got from him was excuses on why he couldn't do something, why he couldn't follow through with something, couldn't find a job, and why he couldn't see a mental health professional for his depression. I finally had to put my foot down and stopped coaching him. It was clear that Farhad didn't want any help, and he didn't want to help himself.

I spoke to a successful Iranian who tried to help Farhad. He said that Farhad wasn't ready to do the hard work required to get to where he needs to be. And no matter what you do, you can't help anyone who doesn't want to be helped.

When I asked him what advice he would give to newcomers, He said, "You have to be flexible! Hold on to your vision and work hard to achieve your goals, But first, you might have to clean dishes or toilets."

Maybe this sounds familiar? I met many "Farhads" and "Alices" in the eleven years I have been in the US. Some were from Eritrea, where I came from, some from Asia, some from other part of Africa, and some from Latin America. It doesn't matter where they are from. Many have lived in the US for more than ten or twenty years. They give excuses for everything. They don't want to adjust even if you are willing to help them; they are always looking for the easy way out, like marrying someone who has been living here and knows the language and who can take care of them. They are so negative, and they would not even care about the person sitting next to them. All their focus is on themselves and their problems.

So what happens when somebody new comes to the US and meets this kind of negative person? They would get the only advice the negative person knows: He/she would say to the newcomer, "Oh, man, the US sucks! You will soon find out that you need to do what you can, man. We have been tricked. We thought coming to America was coming to a country where the money falls off trees. Well, it's not true! You have to work like a mad person, and for what? Nothing! Bills! That's all." He/she would ramble and try to paint his distorted vision of America to the newcomer.

And if the newcomer shared with the negative person their dreams of why they came to America, they would get laughed at and told, "You are kidding. That is not going to happen, man! If that were possible, I would have done it already!" After listening to all of the negative comments, soon, their dreams would start to shrink, and they may start thinking, "Oh my God, this person must be right; after all, they have been here for years, I just arrived, what chance do I have?" They might give up on their dreams even before they start.

Stay away from naysayers. First of all, drop the idea that just because someone has lived in the US for a long time, it means they know everything. That by itself is not a guarantee the person is fully integrated and worked hard to achieve his dreams. When I first came to the US, I thought every person that moved here before me must know everything.

Yes, that's how it should be, and you will find so many well-integrated people who have worked hard and have achieved their dreams. However, not all the people you come in contact with are like that. Look for people you admire, people who encourage you and tell you can make it. Again, stay away from negative people because they will drag you down.

So far, we have looked at your most urgent needs, and how to meet them.

Later in the book, we will come back to those urgent survival needs in-depth, after learning a few essential skills in Chapter Three to help you move to the deep waters. So let's learn some more skillsets and attitudes you need to know to have your dream life manifest in every possible way. All you need is your willingness to learn something new, your determination, and your hard work.

CHAPTER 3

SKILLSET #1: POSITIVE ATTITUDE

"Virtually nothing is impossible in this world if you just put your mind to it and maintain a positive attitude."

LOU HOLTZ

Napoleon Hill's book, Success Through a Positive Mental Attitude, defines a positive mental attitude as comprising the 'plus' characteristics represented by words like faith, integrity, hope, optimism, courage, initiative, generosity, tolerance, tact, kindness, and good common sense.

We understand the definition, but what does a positive attitude look like in everyday life? How do we recognize it?

- Have you ever met someone who made a significant impact on you and lifted you up? You are inspired when you see them looking adversity in the eye, and they keep smiling and laughing.

- Do you have someone in your life who is friendly to strangers and makes everyone around light up?
- Do you have someone in your family you admire because they enjoy their life even when life gives them the unexpected?
- Do you have a motivated friend who is so joyful, and you know for a fact their life is far from perfect?
- Have you met someone so happy with what they have even though what they have is so little?
- Have you met someone who, no matter how hard their life gets or how hard life knocks them down, keeps getting up and lives an inspiring life with honor and grace.

These are a few examples of a positive attitude (also known as a positive mental attitude). People with a positive attitude are fun to be around, they have lots of fun, and because this kind of energy is attractive, they experience a lot of favor from others. Positive people stand out, and they not only live their life with joy, but they bring joy to people around them.

My Grandma, for example, was one of the most positive people I have ever encountered in my life. She would bring calmness to a tense situation. I never heard her say anything bad about anyone. She didn't gossip, and whenever she heard anyone in our family talking about anybody else who was not present, she would lovingly tell us to stop talking about that person. Because the person wasn't present, Grandma said it was gossiping. She wouldn't gossip or complain about anyone, even those who had done her wrong. Because of her loving, nurturing nature, everybody loved my Grandma. She was different from the people around her and refused to participate in anything negative. It's been fourteen years since her passing, and our family, neighbors, and everyone who knew her still think about her and talk of her positiveness. Her attitude is immortal! Growing up, seeing her always expressing love and positive energy, which I believed was unique, intrigued me. I decided early in my life that I wanted to be like her, and to this day, it's who I strive to be.

Some people think we are who we are, and there is nothing we can do to change it. I respectfully disagree! People can change as many times as they want in their lifetime if they put their mind to it. The key is wanting to do it.

However, if someone decides in their heart that they need to change their lifestyle, they can.

It will be more difficult as you grow older and have a set of habits that are not easy to break. We are powerful human beings. Let us not limit ourselves by saying, "we are the way we are." We may have a strong set of habits, but no habit is unbreakable.

People quit smoking, drugs, drinking, and other habits by replacing old habits with new and healthy ones. Strong addictions are hard to break; however, you can break them with new behavioral patterns. Developing new habits takes time. Some experts say habits take about ninety days to form, so if we continuously work on them and are patient with ourselves, we can achieve anything.

Now let's see how a positive attitude can help with your cultural integration process to your new country.

Relocating to a new country and the stress of integrating is a lot to handle. There are a whole bunch of things that can trigger a negative attitude. Here are some examples:

- You need a job, and it is challenging finding work because it's been a while since the last time you have worked.
- You have a higher education, a bachelor's degree, a master's degree, and even a PhD, and the only available jobs are beneath your level. You have to scrub a toilet; you care for the elderly or babysit, and you feel discouraged.
- You are looking for affordable housing, but there is a two-year waiting list.
- You miss your family back home, perhaps you have left your children with plans to get them at a later time, and every minute you are away from them hurts.
- You can't understand a word of the language to communicate in your new country.
- You couldn't get along with your spouse and are now separated, you don't have enough money for the month, and you are worried about how you will make it.
- You couldn't afford the rent, now are sleeping in your car, and trying to keep people from finding out about your current life situation, you have to pretend you are happy while you're hurting inside.

I get it! These are examples of what I have seen some of my clients go through. Life can be upside down like a roller coaster for anyone at any time, and adding the move to a new country, facing a new culture different from what you have been used to, can become triggers for a negative attitude. Then add the current pandemic and the brutal political hostility around us, the racism dialog. And all of that could also trigger you in a way you never expected.

When triggers start hitting, we feel upset and impatient! We may snap at the one trying to help us, or we shout at our child for doing something a child would do. We can't seem to feel happy. When we meet with our friends, we might gossip about other people in a worse situation than us to feel better about ourselves. In return, it drains our energy; it keeps people away from us and doesn't help us progress in life, only triggers a more negative mental attitude. It becomes a never-ending vicious cycle that builds into our behavior and character. And then we end up saying: we are the way we are, and we can't change who we are. However, our attitude is the way it is because knowingly or unknowingly, we chose our attitude and way of life.

Now, let's see how we can be more positive and adopt a positive attitude.

Don't Take Anything Personally

You may have heard this saying a lot and may not understand what it means. Imagine if you didn't take it personally when the person that you had hoped would give you a job doesn't call you back or they hire someone else. Instead of wallowing in self-pity and forming thoughts that say:

- It's because of my accent.
- It's because I am different.

- It's because I'm not the right color.
- I wasn't good enough on the interview.
- The interviewer didn't like me.

These types of thoughts take you into a dark hole you may not be able to come back from.

Instead, if you stop taking things personally, your response might be different. You may think, "Oh well, I hoped I would get this job, but maybe there is something better for me out there. Now I have more interview skills under my belt, and I will do better next time." These thoughts feel good and help you get back in the job-hunting game faster than a negative one would.

Be Flexible

Being flexible is crucial when you move to a new country. It helps if you are willing to let go of what you think should be or shouldn't be. What is right and what's not right. You need to understand that you have a different mentality than the people in the new country because of your upbringing. Refusing to change your mind and your way might make the already painful cultural integration process unbearable. It will keep you in a negative mental attitude of complaining and getting bitter.

Be Accepting

Try to see things from the other's point of view. Think for a second, if an American comes to your country of origin and doesn't speak your language, there would be a lot of misunderstanding between him and the local people. And he might even take offense when someone tries to help. Always keep this image in your mind when you are confused about people or things and give yourself a break. Know you are new here, and you can accept people's way of being even if it is quite different from yours. When you see things from others' points of view, you will refrain from judging the culture and thinking it is wrong. Accept others and their cultures for what it is. It will help you learn more about the culture. Be curious and ask questions to understand instead of condemning and complaining about how wrong the culture is and wanting it to be different.

Some tools and skills can help you improve your mental attitude to integrate into the US culture. There are many; let's talk about them.

As you may have already guessed, everybody loves a positive person. Life is hard for most people, and they want to have peace and warm conversations throughout their day. No one wants to deal with a grumpy person, proving them wrong, or complaining about everything, depleting them of their energy. Most people have enough stress at home or work, and they don't want more pressure added. When they meet and talk to a positive person, it feels uplifting, and they are in a happy place. If you are looking to make a friend to build a support system, a positive attitude will help. If you are trying to get a job, a positive attitude will go beyond education or equivalent experience or training.

When you communicate with others, even if they don't understand your communication, they can feel your positive energy and enjoy being around you. They will go the extra mile to help you with anything you may need.

When I was living in China, I often had contract-based jobs before getting a more permanent position. And I was told by many black people that Chinese people would prefer white teachers no matter what the experience. Every time I went to an interview, I ended up with a job, every single time! Of course, I had the knowledge and experience, but I am willing to bet anything that my positive attitude had something to do with me getting the jobs that many couldn't get.

I was always smiling, interested in the other person, kept everything light and professional. I surveyed this with most people who hired me and found this was true. They were just charmed by my positive attitude and wanted me to be around their students.

People often ask me, "What if I have a difficult situation in my life, and I feel constantly worried, angry, and frustrated? What if I don't feel like it is my job to care about how others feel around me? I don't have time for that and for faking it."

I hear you. It is challenging to be optimistic about life when you have a lot of other challenges. Death of a loved one, your child is sick, you are caregivers to your elderly parents, and you are uncertain about your future. Many things could happen such as your car broke down, you are short of money, divorce, you or your family member diagnosed with an illness, and you don't know what to do, you have family back in your home country that depends on you, you have no idea how to make your life work.

Any of these situations will make you want to cry, get you down, be depressed, and make you feel anxious all the time. The world is full of people who annoy you, careless about others' feelings, insincere people, insensitive people, rude people, angry people, manipulative people, and it can become overwhelming. It's challenging to keep your positive attitude and deal with people while going through all you are going through. I get it! I've been there.

In the above example, when I was interviewing in China as an English teacher, I went through the most difficult time of my life. I had found out my son has a permanent illness that I didn't know how to cope with. Imagine how my job interview would go if I had chosen to bring that up, cry even about the horrible situation I was in, and that I needed a job. Do you think I would get the job? No!

However, I was always learning to manage my emotions during private time with friends and a counselor, and being professional and positive with people at work. It isn't anyone else's job to help us manage our emotions. It's our responsibility to seek the help we need to get support from our friends, loved ones, and even mental health professionals. Although our situation might not change, it's our responsibility to work on our feelings and emotions to feel better and bring ourselves to a positive mentality.

Here are some tips for nurturing and keeping your positive mental attitude when dealing with a difficult situation in your life. It's very natural to respond with shock when something "bad" happens in our lives, and it becomes difficult to think of or talk about anything else. No matter how difficult it may be, step back from, "I can't believe this happened to me." I know it is hard to feel any other way when you concentrate on thoughts like this, but I will ask you to do that. If you are like me, you get so emotional when things beyond our control happen. I am a big crier; I cry, kick, get upset, snap at others, and don't want to get out of bed. These feelings are normal reactions to facing things beyond our control. And to make things worse, if you have not already done a clearing of your emotions work in the past, other negative thoughts will bombard you, pressing on you more. Like, "I am a failure!" "Why are things like this always happening to me?" "I don't see other people struggling with the same things I struggle with; in fact, they look happy and content." "What is wrong with me?" "What did I do in my past life to have all these bad things happen in my life." "God doesn't care or love me. I am cursed."

Before you know it, something powerful has taken over, and your positive light keeps shrinking till all you see is dark and gloomy, and you find yourself anxious or depressed. You don't want to see or talk to other people. You hate your hair; you hate yourself; you might even experience thoughts of suicide. If you have suicidal thoughts frequently and live in the US, please call the National Suicide Prevention Lifeline 1-800-273-8255. If you don't live in the US, please find your National Suicide Prevention Lifeline, and call.

Once we allow our negative thoughts to take us wherever they want, we find ourselves swimming in a vast dark pool. If you find yourself in this place while reading this book and nodding your head, I can assure you this place is familiar to me. I have visited it way too many times, and I am here with a small candlelight in your world to say, "It doesn't have to be this way. You can beat these negative thoughts and climb up to where the light is."

When you find yourself in this situation, I need you to force yourself to write down what you usually love to do. It could be hiking, reading, listening to music, calling and catching up with friends, or getting a massage. Perhaps you like manicure and pedicure, running, walking, praying, no matter what it is, write it down. Once you are finished with your list, look at it, and find one thing that appeals to you and do it. Don't listen to the nagging voice telling you that you don't have time or need to be doing something else. Right now, all that matters is for you to feel better and then great and then greater! Other things can wait. So keep doing things you love till you feel great.

For example, one thing that throws me in a dark mode is when my son Aaron has seizures. No matter what I do, even after sixteen years, I haven't made peace with seizures entirely. How can I? Right? When Aaron goes into a mode of unconsciousness, his eyes turn up, and his little body is shaking and jerking for what seems like forever, although it may be just 50 seconds. I feel my emotions get high with him, and I know I have to focus on caring for him so he doesn't hurt himself.

Once his little body lies still on the ground, helpless, unconscious, gasping for breath, I turn him and lay him down on his side, and make sure he is safe and sleeping. The first thing I do is run to the bathroom and breath heavily and cry. I told you, I am a crier, that is how I let the frustration out of my body.

In the past, while crying, I would allow all kinds of negative thoughts to overtake me. Thoughts like, *what am I going to do? Why can't the doctors and God help him? There is no hope. I failed as a*

91

parent. I am a failure. It's not fair. How can God sit there and do nothing when an innocent child suffers for nothing. I would allow it to take me farther and farther in the darkness. There were days, I kept crying and purposely ignored my friends' calls and ignored my family and walked like a zombie with eyes so heavy with sadness, anger, and hopelessness.

But after many years of torment, I learned to go to the bathroom and feel sad for about ten minutes, sit, breathe, and cry if I feel like it. Then I allow all the old thoughts of negativity to pass through my mind and breathe deeply four or five times, and after another ten minutes, I ask myself one question, "what would make me feel better right now?" I have made several lists over the years, and I know them by heart, to the point that I don't need to look at my list on paper anymore. So, whatever feels right to me at the moment, and if I am in a position to do it, I would get up, wash my face, and do it. It could just be going for a manicure or hiking (if I have someone to care for my son); maybe it is just praying in my bedroom, watching a funny movie with my son next to me. Whatever I love to do at the moment, it will snap me out of my negative thoughts.

Once I have gained my natural state, I would purposely feel my thoughts positively, building only on the good. I would say positive things about Aaron to myself. For example, *"my son is doing well, he didn't break his neck in the process, and he is the happiest person I know."* This mentality keeps me in touch with my boy and gives me thoughts of what to do for him when he wakes up. Plan something fun with him, watching a movie, reading his favorite book, eating something delicious, or playing his favorite music.

92

Most importantly, right after a seizure, Aaron goes to sleep because he is tired from all the jerking. I use this time to feel the negative emotions that come to me, remove them, replace them with positive thoughts with the power of prayer, or do something that makes me happy. When he wakes up, he sees his happy mom instead of a stressed-out mom crying and complaining. The negative emotions will not help my son, but they will make him feel sad and bad because he can't control the seizures.

The importance of gaining control of your negative thoughts is crucial no matter how hard your mind wants you to wallow in the problem. You will be able to calm yourself and be present in your life in a powerful way. If you find yourself in this kind of situation now or in your future, no matter what caused this situation, try the method I mentioned to snap yourself out of your situation so that you can approach your problem with a positive and cheerful heart.

Please note that the exercise may take a while to master, but don't get discouraged if it doesn't work for you when you try for the first time. Just keep going at it. Keep repeating the exercise every time, and if you reach for the ice cream, that's okay. Forgive yourself and move on. The next time you will choose a positive habit from your list. By being consistent, you will have mastered your emotional state before you know it, even when something horrible is happening in your life. Like I said before, all things worth learning will take time to master. Sometimes a lifetime, but just take baby steps towards it consistently.

I don't consider myself a master, as I am still on the path of learning. There are times; I feel sad, angry, hopeless, and some days it may take me longer to recover and come back to my happy self. There are situations that I didn't expect that knock me down off my center. When I fail, I keep going back to the tools to help me return to my positive self. Don't think that once you are embracing the exercises, you will be immune from any negative situations. We are human, we will never be perfect. However, we can always go back to our toolbox. Every time we go back to our learned tools, it gets better and better, and the time that takes you to go back to being positive gets shorter and shorter. It is a journey. The tools above are just examples that work perfectly for me. You can find many resources and information on achieving a positive attitude while struggling with life's challenges.

Invest your time and block off some time every week to learn more about it and practice having a positive attitude. Here are some examples you can try:

- Smile at two or three people per day when you're out.
- Strike up a light conversation with a stranger.
- When your kids drive you crazy, instead of reacting and shouting at them (we've all been there more than once), try speaking gently with a smile or give them a hug.

Life provides us with opportunities that are challenging. We can practice using these moments as our chance to work on having a positive attitude in the face of life's difficult trials.

CHAPTER 4

SKILLSET #2: HEALTHILY MANAGING YOUR EMOTIONS

"Our emotions play a vital role in living a happy, healthy, and a successful life. All emotions, from love and joy, to anger and fear, have an important part to play in understanding ourselves and others. They help us discover the wonders of this life as well as warn us when we are in danger. But this diversity of feelings is meant to complement our life, not determine it."

—JOYCE MEYER

According to Dr. Neil Levitsky, MD, FRCPC Psychiatrist, there are two types of emotions: positive and negative. Positive feelings consist of joy, love, and peace of mind. Negative feelings consists of anger and fear.

For this book's purpose, we will focus on the negative emotions because they are the ones we need to learn to manage.

Major Types of Negative Emotions

The following are the four main categories/types of negative emotions:

- Sadness (depression, despair, hopelessness)
- Anxiety (fear, worry, concern, nervous, panic)
- Anger (irritation, frustration, annoyance, rage)
- Guilt (shame, embarrassment)

Note: *Generally, any time a person feels negative emotions, it could be classified into one of the five "flavors" (and more than one could be experienced at the same time).*

Source: http://cognitivetoronto.com/Cognitive_Toronto

Anger

Anger is a powerful emotion and even scary at times because its manifestation can be intense. Most cultures discourage its expression. Growing up, I used to hear these common phrases, "Don't be angry," "You don't need to be angry," "Stop being angry," Being angry in front of others is bad." As a result, I never learned how to express my anger positively.

It wasn't only anger I wasn't allowed to feel, but also sadness, and that it's not ok to show frustration because it's not good manners. Most of the time, there were social consequences for expressing those feelings, so I felt like I had to hide all my negative emotions from everyone.

I hid them because they seemed dangerous, and I thought it was something to put out right away like a fire. Not having control of those emotions was considered inappropriate. So, instead of understanding my feelings, allowing them to surface, and managing them, I learned how to stuff them inside and I became good at that.

Holding feelings becomes a problem because they have to come out at some point. Imagine emotions like an ocean with all its mystery, and you try to contain it or build a dam to control it. When the wind blows, or it rains, the ocean overflows regardless of the boundaries constructed around it.

In my experience, I felt like I mastered suppressing all the fear, anger, sadness, and frustration I felt for at least a year. The problem was that those feelings had limitations, and I didn't know where the limits were, and once in a while, my emotions would surprise me and others around me. At that point, I would be scared because they were so intense, just like an ocean. I might blow up for the smallest thing, but what usually would happen is I would feel angry about all the feelings that I stuffed before and with all the pressure and stress that would trigger in me. It would take little to push me emotionally over the edge. I would emotionally explode. And God help the person who triggered my anger, usually left shocked and confused by my overreaction with such intensity, for such what appeared to be a "small thing." They would not understand that I wasn't just angry about that particular thing they said or did. All the same, it triggered me to a giant blow-up of anger that I hadn't dealt with, and that "small thing" they said or did was like permission for all of it to blow up.

What can I tell you, when the explosion happened, it was like shaken champagne that sends a cork flying into someone's head and a fountain of bubbles to the kitchen floor. I tell you; it was a mess.

As a teenager, I often remember being challenged; I lacked the understanding of how to control the shaking, the crying, the shouting, and getting physical if the person had physically provoked me. After the anger subsided, I would feel ashamed and thought I was a failure because I couldn't control my feelings in front of others. How crazy is that?

The same happened with my feelings of sadness and frustration. Mostly my triggers ignited when someone did something I didn't expect. Such as a friend betraying my trust in any way, or when in a situation where I have to handle multiple tasks simultaneously or get so stressed out I would go into retreat mode. I would feel depressed for a few days and physically sick, and possibly I would have to take a day off from school or work to take care of myself. I would feel all the sadness that I had been refusing to feel. Most of the time, a day or two would take care of it. I would feel overwhelmed, similar to how I feel whenever I have to clean and organize my home after a long time, not knowing where to start. I usually feel overwhelmed and stash things away; it doesn't matter where I put them as long as I don't see them around anymore. Out of sight, out of mind. Right? But only till it gets messy again, and then I would be forced to deal with it again and again. It's the reason I learned to clean and organize as often as possible; otherwise, I know I would feel overwhelmed. And after many years, I learned how to manage my negative feelings.

I learned a coping skill that allowed me to compartmentalize my thoughts, feelings, and emotions. I dealt with urgent feelings that needed my attention and put the rest away in a box in my mind. Somehow, I convinced myself that I would deal with it when it's convenient for me since I have to function in the world. I thought this method was ingenious, and it is a surviving skillset, so many people use it, but soon I would discover that didn't work either.

Finally, I met Clara, an excellent social worker who helped me understand my feelings and let me know I didn't need to be scared of them. And thanks to her, I was introduced to the world of managing emotions. I learned to feel various types of emotions, whether it was anger or sadness or frustration, and healthily dealt with them without the emotional explosions. I learned to let them go and go about my day.

Healthily dealing with my emotions is like taking a shower, a "soul shower," I call it. I never understood why we, most humans, no matter where we are born, don't teach our kids how to deal with their feelings and emotions when they are young at home, at school, since it is one of the most crucial lessons of life. I'm not sure if I will ever understand it, but I know without it, our relationships, friendships, and family relations will suffer.

Please take heed, coming to the US; you will have many feelings and emotions, from sadness to anger, from hopelessness to deep depression during the process of cultural integration. Unless you are one of the very few lucky ones taught how to deal with negative emotions before you arrived, like the rest of us, you must learn how to manage your feelings, manage your life, and work on your goals to achieve your American dream.

When Anger Turns to Domestic Violence

I feel like it's worth talking about domestic violence as I see many cases in court that relate to that. I want to start by telling you a story.

One day, when I was living in Africa, I was walking to meet a friend at a café, and as I was walking, I was thinking of the great news to share with her about me moving to the US. However, I diverted my attention to the couple walking in front of me. I could tell they were arguing.

I immediately thought about my relationship with my boyfriend at the time and how our arguments sometimes escalated too loud. We would both try to argue our point, and as much as I hate arguing, it seemed to resolve issues misunderstood by both of us.

So, I looked at the couple and smiled at them, understanding the dynamics of what it takes for a relationship to work when suddenly, the man slapped the woman so hard on the face twice that I heard the sound although they were a few feet away from me. Although it was not the first time I saw people hitting one another when upset, I was shocked. I even got into physical fights in my high school years. I had seen guys hit a girl before, and it got me so rattled, it triggered childhood trauma. I automatically went into a defense mode. I ran to rescue the woman. She was crying, holding her hand on her cheek and mumbling something. The guy calmed down, talking to her softly, I guess, trying to give her his point of view. I was angry, and I shouted, "Hey, what the hell do you think you are doing hitting a girl?" He looked and ignored me, which made me furious, and I said, "I am talking to you. Why don't you pick on someone your size?" I was ready to punch him, although he was twice my size. He told me to mind my own business. I replied, "You made it my business when you took your violent behavior out in the street." At this point, I got his attention, and I saw the anger in his eyes. Although I was terrified and scared inside, still, I was ready to punch him once or twice, even if I got hurt in the process. I thought I could teach that moron a lesson that he probably never learned because the women in his life didn't confront him.

Suddenly, the woman looked at me with spite and told me to mind my own business, "cussed" me out of my name, embarrassed me, and almost wanted to punch me asking me to leave her and her man alone. Very surprised, I left, feeling so small, shamed, and disempowered, mumbling things like, "Wow, you can't stand up for yourself, and you also shame people who dare to stand up for you? Wow!" I talked about it with my friend over a cappuccino and family and friends for the rest of the week. I have argued about this situation with both men and women from my community. Some people told me the same thing my family and neighbors had been telling me when I got into a fight with a boy when I was a kid. I would fight a boy for provoking me and come home to complain about it, and they would tell me not to fight a boy again. After all, he didn't provoke me because he didn't like me but because he probably "liked" me. To this day, I still don't get it. Hitting doesn't display love! And I believe no culture should teach their little girls to take abuse in the name of "love."

If you come from a similar cultural belief as I did, I challenge you to challenge that belief system. This kind of cultural belief encourages a girl to grow up and put up with men who will mistreat, use, and abuse her. She will tolerate these behaviors and will think it is an expression of love. On the other hand, a boy will learn that the way to display his love is to mistreat and abuse women. I have told this story and retold it many times, and surprisingly, I have met some American women who told me they had experienced the same things in their childhood.

Some people from the culture I came from agreed with my point of view, and some thought I was crazy or acting modern and like westerners since I had this belief even before moving to the US.

After I moved to America, one day, I was at the courthouse in Santa Clara County to interpret for a case. As I usually do, I went to the interpreters' office to get the paperwork. I typically don't get to know about the case other than basic information about the case name, time, type of violation, and department number. I got the paperwork and sat down with my spicy tea to see what kind of case I was going to interpret for. Sure enough, I found out it was a domestic violence case. It was around the time when I first started my job as a court interpreter. Although I saw many domestic violence cases in my ten-year plus career. This one stood out because it was my first time to interpret for that kind of case in the US. So, as you can imagine, I was already tensing up.

The case was typical, a husband and wife got into an argument, and it escalated where the husband got physical, the wife screamed, and neighbors called the police. It was the first time the couple appeared in court. The husband was out of police custody and dressed nicely. It was a pre-trial conference, and his court-appointed defense attorney advised the defendant (the husband) to come back another day so he could have more time to investigate. After the case was over, I ran into the defendant in the elevator. The defendant said, "thank you for helping me out with interpreting." He looked so confused and shocked, and then he said, "it was just a small fight. What was the big deal? I love my wife; I was angry, and I slapped her. What was the problem? It was between my wife and me. Why am I being called to the courthouse? What do you think they are going to do? They know she is my wife. We love each other; I love my wife so much."

I was shocked. For the first time in my life, I was able to see men in a new light in the way the culture raised them, just like us women were. At that moment, my anger disappeared. I understood his dilemma and had compassion for his shock and confusion. Raised in his culture, learning it was okay to hit a girl, he came to another culture that punishes that kind of crime.

Who do we blame? I have studied cultures, and I respect cultures, but every culture has its good and bad practices. American culture isn't an exception. I don't care which culture you belong to; hitting a woman in the name of love falls to the harmful practice of culture. We should not tolerate domestic violence; we must fight against it like all other bad cultural practices.

When I was growing up, neighbors would go to the couple's house with the problem and resolve the matter when domestic violence happened. If they saw the man was too harsh, they would tell him to ease up on the beating. Mind you, not forbidding the hitting, since hitting was perceived as a sign of love once in a while. But in Western countries, there is no such thing as resolving your issue with relatives and neighbors' help, it's a matter of the law, and actually, violence against another is a felony. It can ruin your life, and your family's once you have it on your record.

So, you can imagine when the police came for this poor guy, his whole world turned upside down, and he didn't know what to think or feel. He was horrified, confused, and felt like an outsider: everyone knew what he was and wasn't supposed to do except him. Poor guy! I'm sure he learned his lesson after the judge ordered him to attend a domestic violence class. I hope he eventually learned how to manage his emotions and healthily express them and thrive in his new country. And to find a new way to express his love to his wife.

All violence is terrible but domestic violence is the most common one and something you need to be aware of. Learning to manage your emotions, especially anger, is important.

There are classes online and offline, many books you can pick up to help you learn how to manage anger and other negative emotions. It's better to start training yourself instead of dealing with it once your emotions get you in trouble in smaller or more significant ways. There is one more sad story I want to share before moving on to the next topic.

It was a domestic violence and attempted murder case. A man, who is an immigrant from a developing country, angry with his wife, stressed and frustrated; while working with a hammer, hit his wife right in the head with it. Luckily for the wife, although she was knocked unconscious, she didn't die or suffer a brain injury.

This man was arrested and faced 12 years in prison. He pleaded not guilty against his attorney's advice due to the strong evidence against him. The saddest part is, we noticed the lack of remorse in his behavior. This person felt that he was wrongly accused and should be released. He thought he would be able to fix his relationship with his wife. The wife said clearly in her testimony that she didn't even want to see him again, let alone live with him. She was obviously terrified of him. Even after hearing the wife's testimony, he still didn't recognize the magnitude and impact his behavior had on his family and future.

He was shocked when the jury found him guilty. He was so amazed he started blaming his lawyer. Sometimes, the way we're raised has a stronghold over us; we can't even push through it to see new ideas and new concepts. And we can't see ourselves and our actions outside of the image we hold of how life should be according to our upbringing and personality. It's a sad story. He felt that maybe he overdid it a little using a hammer, but he felt like it still was not a big deal to fight with his wife and that it shouldn't be enough to put him in prison. He expected he could make things right.

Of course, this is an extreme case, and we might not find ourselves in this kind of situation, and I hope we don't; however, letting our emotions get a hold of us might get us in trouble one way or another if we don't learn how to manage them.

Emotions are Complicated

Moving to the US, one of the most challenging parts of understanding your emotions and figuring out what different emotions you may be feeling is sorting out the words associated with them. Stress, anxiety, frustration, overwhelm, worry, the list goes on, aren't they the same? Apparently not! Especially if you are like me and didn't grow up talking about emotions. Perhaps it took you years to make peace with Americans having so many words to explain feelings and wanting to label and diagnose everything. That was one of my culture shocks.

The most common feelings that we feel in a new country are stress and anxiety.

According to Neurocore Brain Performance Center, both stress and anxiety can trigger a very physical response, which can make differentiating the two confusing. Rapid heartbeat, shaking hands, and dry mouth, for example, are all classic symptoms of anxiety and stress.

There are, however, a couple of ways to help differentiate between stress and anxiety. One way is that with stress, there's a known source— you're on a tight deadline, or the kids just won't listen. Alternatively, people with an anxiety disorder will frequently be anxious for no apparent reason.

Another aspect of anxiety is often the degree to which symptoms are felt. Being anxious without an obvious cause can trigger a snowball effect, leaving people anxious about feeling anxious. It can become a normal state of being for some people—waking up feeling anxious, going to work feeling nervous, running errands feeling anxious. Adding stressors added into the mix can exacerbate those physical symptoms to the point of a panic attack.

Also, know that being overwhelmed is notably different than having a panic attack. A panic attack's symptoms can vary depending on the person, but many people describe the feeling as having a heart attack. Some of the more common symptoms include:

- *Racing heart*
- *Feeling weak, faint, or dizzy*
- *Tunnel vision*
- *Trembling*
- *Tingling or numbness in the hands and fingers*
- *Sense of terror, or impending doom, or death*
- *Feeling sweaty or having chills*
- *Chest pains*
- *Breathing difficulties*
- *Feeling a loss of control*

*Source: https://www.neurocorecenters.com
/blog/am-i-stressed-or-anxious*

When you move to a new country your whole world may shift. Although you are excited to come to a new country, you will most likely feel like someone removed the rug under your feet. It's an extremely uncomfortable feeling.

If you don't speak the language well enough, sometimes you may feel silly bubbling like a kid in front of a schoolteacher, you feel inadequate and try to disguise how you feel by being angry or rude. Maybe you have mastered the language, but words fail you when you try to express your feelings and emotions and feel frustrated. You may easily tear up because you can't tell the person what you want them to understand. Depending on how you deal with frustration, you may tear up and respond in anger because the person you interact with doesn't know what you are trying to communicate. The other person has no idea what is going on in your inner world. All they may see is this person from another country is being rude, crying, and arguing with them in anger, and they have no idea why. Their decision isn't going to be, "oh my God, this person is new here and might be feeling frustrated," instead, they would get defensive. They would withdraw or decide to withhold a piece of essential information to get back at you.

Wherever you go, you may run into challenges, such as:

- Language barrier
- Figuring out the behavior of your coworkers
- Dealing with racism, with no idea how to handle it
- Trying to find affordable housing
- Moving to another city
- You are dealing with finding a new job, and the co-workers seem to act "weird" or different, and you don't know how to deal with that.

- Maybe your neighbors aren't friendly, although you are always friendly to them. In your home country, neighbors are like an extended family.

- In your new country, people might seem rude; they don't say hello, and if they do, it's only a brief hello. They would ask, "How are you doing?" but they would not stay around to hear your answer.

- You may have problems with the law. A police officer stopped you for allegedly saying hello to the little cute baby girl you saw in the park, and you kissed her on the cheek. It is a practice that is being polite and expected in your culture. However, it is not customary in your new country. Now you face charges that could complicate your life for giving a friendly kiss to a cute baby girl, and you are trying to understand everything happening around you as if you were a kid.

- You go to the grocery store to buy bread and milk, and it takes you an hour or sometimes two to figure out which options to buy from a hundred gazillion options available on the shelves. Your eyes are watering, trying to read the small, fine type under every item, but no one is there to help you. You want to know what the difference is, and you decide on one. Then you look at the price and choose to buy the cheapest brand. You're now wondering why there is such a difference in prices when bread is bread and milk is milk until you discover after arriving home that the milk you bought tastes like water.

  You question yourself if the grocery store robbed you and if they gave you water instead of milk. After the milk episode, you would now be afraid to go to the grocery store. You feel bad that you have to bother your sponsor, a friend, or a caseworker to ask a simple question: What is the best milk to buy?

Your days/incidents may not be as dramatic as those I just mentioned, which are true stories of people I interviewed. You get the idea. At first, when you arrive in your new country, sorting out your life and dealing with day-to-day challenges may be overwhelming.

Honestly, I am feeling overwhelmed writing all of the above and remembering the times I had to juggle so many things in a single day in a culture full of people I didn't understand.

Sometimes things went my way, and I came home feeling all pumped-up. But most of the time, I came back home tired, defeated, with my head down, rushing through dinner, getting my boy to sleep before I could finally take a shower and squeeze in a little "me time," where I could de-stress.

Afterward, I would squeeze in research and reading time to learn something new, brushing up my language and people skills. So yes, I do get it! So, how do you manage all of this newness in life you have got going for yourself?

And by the way, if you are one of the lucky ones, who have family members already culturally integrated before you arrived, I congratulate you. Probably you have skipped most of the overwhelming tasks since you have a strong support system already in place, and your family is explaining to you the steps to take, pointing you in the right direction if you need the extra resource.

Managing your emotions takes time, patience, and practice and most of us never learned how to manage our feelings growing up. Even in the US, some people grew up in a culture or household where talking about emotions isn't something you do. Even our parents or neighbors might not have talked about the overwhelming emotions. We just stumbled and watched how our parents, neighbors, and friends dealt with feelings. We unconsciously copied their coping mechanisms. We react to life and situations as we are conditioned. Sometimes, that works, and other times it causes us grief and frustration because it doesn't work.

The Curse of Being Exceptionally Strong

Being labeled as "super-strong" has its disadvantage. People will lean on you and tell you their problems because they want to relate to you, which is such an honor; however, if you haven't dealt with your inner demons (negative emotions), it is a burden.

In my case, it became a burden because some people felt they had permission to tell me their problems, which in turn made me more anxious and depressed. And I thought I couldn't refuse to listen because in their mind I was such a strong person I could handle their problems, and I didn't want to disappoint them. After all, I handled my significant life challenges with flying colors, so their problems would be a piece of cake. I often shared how I learned to cope with my problems while giving them ideas on how to cope with theirs. And they would thank me and go home feeling lighter and happier, while I felt depleted, tired, and more anxious than before I listened to their challenges.

Helping people with their challenges was the birth of my gift. Many people started telling me I should be a counselor, a psychologist, write a book, or be a minister. At that time, I laughed at those comments and thanked them, but I sincerely thought I would never do that. Why would anyone want to carry someone else's burden?

It seemed that everyone in my life expected me to be strong for them. However, I didn't think I had anyone willing to be strong for me and allow me to break down every once in a while. Or recognize that I am human and have feelings and emotions like everybody else.

I remember praying and asking God to give me friends who can handle my emotions when I am not strong enough. I also prayed and asked Him to help me win a lottery to buy an island retreat just for me and hire people to care for my son: whenever I feel overwhelmed and weak; I can leave everyone behind and be on the island by myself, screaming if I needed to, or crying, with no one around to disappoint me or judge me. And the ocean and the blue sky would comfort me. It was a perfect fantasy.

I don't know where you are in the world right now, but if you nod and relate to what I am talking about, don't worry; there is hope for you like there was hope for me.

I didn't win the lottery; other than that, God answered my prayers. Slowly people started showing up in my life who not only could handle my breakdowns or share my vulnerability, but they could also relate to what I was feeling. I found two amazing counselors who have helped me understand my feelings and healthily manage them. And how to communicate what I needed and how I wanted to be treated when I needed emotional support.

The more I learned to unload and deal with the grief I was feeling for my son, the more I could see clearly. My energy came back, and I radiated positive energy; however, I wasn't faking it this time. With a lot of work on myself, reading books that helped me understand more about emotions and feelings, and developing and using my already established hobbies to cope with my feelings, I was able to feel happier in my life. I became a better mom to my son (who is indeed my teacher and Guru), a better daughter, a better sister, and a better friend. It took many years, but I sure felt lighter, and instead of using my energy to stuff my feelings and emotions and hide them from everyone, I had so much energy left for me to build my life and my son's the way I wanted it.

I even started understanding what people meant when talking about my "gifts," and I started coaching many people who crossed my path. It was the birth of my coaching business. Through coaching people, I gained understanding. I started being genuinely interested in people and what was going on with them. I started understanding the human connection through the pain. I learned how to honor everyone's problem, no matter how big or small. I learned to establish meaningful and lasting friendships that were authentic. I was having breakthroughs where I struggled before.

I learned how to really listen to people without making it about me. I didn't know how to do that before; I used to just fake it. I also learned to love people, be happy, and share their happiness about whatever happy milestone they were having in their lives.

True Freedom/Unload Your Baggage

When you unload your pain, frustration, and all the feelings you have been firmly and honorably holding onto, you will find that life is terrific. But we must always free ourselves to enjoy true freedom. If you want to enjoy freedom, you must do the work. I mean the healing work.

You need to unload your emotional baggage, just as you would your luggage when coming back from travel. No matter what you have gone through, with the right help, right friends, and proper support, you can free yourself. And, when you do, you will taste the sweetness of true freedom. True freedom can't be explained, and no one can give it to you because it is yours to take, and when you feel it, you will wake up one day and say, "Oh, wow, this must be freedom."

Earlier in the chapter, I talked about healthy ways of managing feelings and emotions. Below is a list of unhealthy ways of not managing your emotions. This list will give you an idea of where you are and how you can assess a new way of managing your emotions.

It's normal to find yourself not healthily managing your emotions. You may find yourself in this category most times. And when you do, the first reaction might be shame, guilt, or denial; it's all ok. No one teaches us how to communicate healthily, so we all start in the same boat, and when I say we, I mean most of humanity in general, regardless of where you were born and raised. It isn't taught in school, not even in college. And while growing up, we don't have the chance to learn it either. It's something you learn through practice and experience throughout your life. Mostly by trial and error in friendships, marriage, and other types of relationships.

Unhealthy ways of NOT managing your emotions:

- Smoking
- Drinking
- Being violent
- Being manipulative
- Self-sabotaging
- Throwing adult tantrum
- Sex addiction
- Anger
- Frustration

When we don't know how to handle our emotions, we express them negatively. Below are some tried and true methods you may use to help eliminate unhealthy behavior:

- First, identify the emotion. What are you feeling? Anger? Sadness? Frustration? Overwhelm? Don't run away from it; feel it.
- Second, accept your emotions. Say to yourself: "I feel angry," "I feel frustrated," "I feel overwhelmed." Identifying and accepting your feelings will help you, and you can let them go.
- Third, find the source of your emotions. Why are you angry? Was it that rude person you encountered who said something

that upset you? Or are you frustrated about your child who is being difficult? Are you overwhelmed because you have a lot of things to do and so little time? Identify what it is.

- Fourth, let go, or change, or take care of what is causing the emotions. There are some things you can change or let go of to feel better about your feelings. If you are upset about that rude encounter, you can acknowledge that the person was rude; maybe he was upset about something or didn't mind his manners. Just let it go unless this person is someone you regularly see; in that case, you can talk to that person, and maybe find out what happened that made them behave the way they did. If they are still rude, tell them you don't appreciate being treated like that, maintain your distance, and let it go. If they apologize for offending you, make peace and let it go.

If you are frustrated about your child, seek help, ask your friends, teachers, and counselors to help you find a solution. The very act of taking action will make you feel better. When you are overwhelmed about too many things on your plate, ask others to help you with some of the tasks. You could ask your partner and your kids to help out with some of the household tasks. Learn about time management. Again, the very act of taking action will help you feel better.

A friend once told me that she overeats when she feels overwhelmed. "I can't help it," she said. I was happy when my friend eventually learned to manage her anxiety and took action to learn time management skills and the art of delegation—and stopped overeating when she felt overwhelmed. It is possible to adopt healthy coping skills and replace unhealthy and damaging behavior.

The last step is to repeat the steps. Practice makes perfect.

Every time you feel an intense emotion, don't run to anger, overeating, drinking, or other unhealthy behaviors; face your feelings head-on, feel them, accept them, identify the source, and take action or let go. And repeat. Building healthy habits requires consistency and repetition. Like all skills, it needs to be developed. You will have to work hard to establish new habits and break bad patterns. It's not easy, but you can do it. Emotions are part of our lives, both positive and negative, and we can never avoid them.

Sometimes we go from happiness to sadness to depression to joy in one day. Our thoughts are connected to our emotions. Our thoughts create our feelings. Studies show we have between 50,000–70,000 thoughts per day; this means between 35 and 48 thoughts per minute per person. You can imagine how many different emotions we feel per day that comes along with every thought. So what we think creates feelings and emotions in us. Most of it imagined.

I met Sarah, a sweet 68 years old woman, a very traditional woman from Somalia. She told me that she had trouble sleeping. And I asked her why she laughed and said, "What do you mean why? I can't control what happens; I can only pray and hope things get better." Then I said, "You are right about the prayer because that is helpful, but let's explore why you are not sleeping."

She was willing to try to explore with me, so I asked her, "Are you worried about something?" She said, "Of course, I am a human being.

I worry." Then I asked, "What do you worry about, especially at night?" She thought about it for a bit and told me that she misses her children back in Africa. Some of them were married and had their lives. Two of her daughters, both in their 20's, weren't. And she thought about them a lot.

"That's normal. I can't imagine being away from my kids, and I would miss them too. But what are you worried about specifically?"

"I fear something bad is going to happen to them. Sometimes, I have visions that my daughter gets hit by a car, and I am jumpy when people call me in the evening or early morning. I fear they are calling me to confirm that something terrible has happened to my son. I fear one of my daughters might get pregnant without being married. I fear they may have gotten themselves in an accident. I sometimes am so scared of the images I see in my head, that I get up in the morning without having slept very much."

"How long have you had those images in your mind?" "It's been ten years."

"That's a long time. Has any of those images come true?"

Sarah jumped and said, "Oh no, my goodness, why would you even think of that?"

"If you don't want them to come true, why do you keep entertaining them in your mind, sometimes the entire night?"

Sarah looked puzzled, and I saw a light bulb go on, and finally, she said, "Because I can't control it."

"Is that true? What happens if you divert your thoughts to prayer or good wishes when you have those images? Those images are a creation of your worried mind. We can create different images in our minds that create good feelings."

"Would you like your daughters to get married?"

Sarah's face lit up. "Of course! That's my dream!"

"So, now imagine your daughters getting married, and you are dancing next to them, and everyone is smiling." She did, and her face showed a huge smile and happiness.

"Could you try to replace the horrifying images that come up?" She said she would do that and also agreed to pray whenever those scary images came up. We both were smiling at the end.

Sarah and I met a few years later at a mutual friend's wedding and she told me that the talk had changed her life. She shared that sometimes she was still anxious, but it was not happening as often as before; she was more relaxed and sleeping well. and occasionally takes sleeping pills. Sarah looked more comfortable and at ease. She told me that she keeps practicing the skill of changing her mental screen to nicer images when bad thoughts about her kids come to mind. And her friends were helping her with prayers, keeping up her faith, and she even went to visit her kids in her home country, where she enjoyed her time with them before coming back to the US.

I was so happy to see her smile and laugh while talking to me and others around her. She was freer from her debilitating condition. Just by doing such a simple practice, she enjoyed her life more and was happier.

Throughout the day, we think, and we react to those thoughts. I don't think it is humanly possible not to think about them entirely;

however, it's up to us which "wolf" to feed. Why not think positive thoughts and feel at peace instead of thinking about something that is not true and create worry? It's so important that we master how to take hold of our emotions instead of letting our feelings and emotions have a hold of us.

CHAPTER 5

SKILLSET #3: BEING OPEN TO A LIFETIME OF LEARNING

This skill set is essential since, without growth and learning, nothing is possible. When we were kids, we had to take steps to become the adults that we are today. First, as babies, we must start creeping and crawling before we walk. We creep so many times before we master it, and when we do, we experiment with crawling. We crawl several times, sometimes for days and months before we master it. And then we try standing up, and we must practice walking for several days and months before we master it, and then we attempt to run.

By design, usually, to learn things, we must practice, master, and take on the next challenge. But for most of us, sometimes, we stop growing and get stuck somewhere in life. Occasionally, we graduate from college, get a job, and think that our learning is over.

Sometimes we get married, have babies, and stop learning. Our attention is taken by raising honorable kids, and mastering parenting is the best thing ever and the most difficult. But often, we lose ourselves in a job, parenting, or responsibility. We may forget the lifetime learning process: Do something repeatedly, become a master at it, and try something new.

Just because we grew up, got a job, got married, or had children, learning doesn't stop. Striving for something more, something challenging that we have never tried, is in our DNA. Learning new things and trying something challenging is how we grow. We expand our minds. When we keep learning and challenging ourselves, it doesn't add to our busyness as much as it adds value to our lives. We become better parents, better employees; our brain stays sharp and focused on getting us going. Without the willingness to learn and grow consistently, we stall and become very rigid in our thinking.

Wikipedia defines lifelong learning as follows.

Lifelong learning is the ongoing, voluntary, and self-motivated pursuit of knowledge for either personal or professional reasons. Therefore, it not only enhances social inclusion, active citizenship, and personal development, but also self-sustainability, as well as competitiveness and employability.
Source: https://en.wikipedia.org/wiki/Lifelong_learning

In most cultures, going to school, getting a degree, and maybe your master's and doctorate is a noble thing to do. The more formal education you have, the more respect you will have from your community. Formal education is essential, and when you come to your new country, you have many choices to study and be whoever you want to be, build a career you love, and get a job to sustain your life financially. Formal education is a vehicle for that.

I love education. I completed my bachelor's degree in Sociology and Anthropology after I graduated from high school. I also went to a bio-health college when I moved to California and got my diploma in bio-health.

I have already built my career as a court interpreter and cultural integration mentor, author, and speaker; it has always been a dream of mine to get my graduate degree. It is on the list for me.

However, the learning I am referring to in this chapter is mostly about learning outside of formal education. I am talking about informal or self-guided education.

I will never understand why traditional education doesn't include the most critical part of learning about life. It is vital to our survival once we live our lives as independent adults, to learn about friendship, relationships and marriage, money management, and how to be happy—to mention a few. Most of us learn about those critical parts of life by watching others. As life gets complicated, we soon know that we don't have the tools to handle what life throws at us.

Even if we have a college degree, we don't necessarily feel equipped to handle and maintain friendships. We see our marriage is not working, so we wonder why we don't know how to handle it. We start blaming ourselves. I have heard people say, "How come she or he isn't handling their marriage, they're educated. Aren't educated people supposed to know how to manage their lives?"

You might say we learn important parts of our lives in churches. That is true; I have learned about forgiveness, being a good person, and all that. When I was a kid, I attended Catholic school during the summer and sang spiritual songs and all that, yet I don't remember practical lessons for current living issues that I need with friends, neighbors, and others.

My mom used to take me to her church (Orthodox); the ceremony was in an ancient language that no one understood, but everyone recited. And I still respect those ceremonies. There is peace and love that you experience when you are in that setting. However, I didn't get a more practical education about life lessons there, either.

In school, you learn different fascinating things. You may learn to fly an airplane, how to do electrical work, to care for patients when they get sick. You may even learn how to go to the moon and study other planets. It's really captivating!

However, learning those skills doesn't guarantee you will have healthy, lasting friendships, a happy marriage; the ability to get along with your coworkers and your surroundings. It doesn't guarantee you will be happy in life. It doesn't tell you how to avoid bad habits and addictions or how to break them. It doesn't teach you how to raise your kids to be decent human beings or manage your money and save—all important lessons that are so vital for our existence.

In school, kids may learn to become an astronomer, doctor, lawyer, or other career dreams they may have. Still, school does not prepare them to stand up to bullies, does not teach girls how to handle boys or boys how to treat girls, and face other challenges that come at that age.

Sometimes, in worst-case scenarios, not being able to handle social pressures, even in schools with counseling available, may cost a young person their life.

It seems formal education only gives you half of the skills you need to survive life. Which is probably why social problems are all we talk about with our friends and hear on the media. We are social animals, so no matter what we're trained to do in life, we must live with others. And not having the right skills to cope with every stage of your life could be very costly, or deadly in the worst scenarios.

When I first started as a court interpreter eight years ago, I saw many criminal cases: some heartbreaking, some that led me to believe they were committed due to cultural integration problems, and some that taught me lessons. I am so grateful for my job because I learned a lot about interpreting, US social issues, and US laws. I love, and I am proud of my job because it has not only given me money and a career, but wisdom and a new perspective in culture, integration, social problems, and so much more.

I have seen many defendants charged with a misdemeanor where the defendant pleads guilty. That's because sometimes the defendant gets some corrective education as part of his plea bargain. Those education programs include domestic violence classes, AA meetings, therapy, drug programs, counseling, parenting classes, and many more. The defendant is not finished until he/she shows proof that they have completed the program that the judge ordered. Some defendants return month after month until they complete the program to satisfy the court's wishes.

I have taken some programs myself as part of my job's continuing education, and I can't tell you how much the programs have helped me in my life. It makes me wonder why our education system doesn't include similar educational classes to help us learn early on how to cope with life before we get into trouble. Why do we have to get into trouble before we know what would help us not get into trouble? It doesn't make sense to me. But the world is what it is. So it is up to us to be proactive and educate ourselves.

Because there is no formal education system that gives us this vital informational education, it usually falls in the hands of great families, religious institutions, and social groups. These groups educate children, who become adults making contributions to their society and the world in extraordinary ways; however, it's not always the case.

I don't have to get you research and survey data to prove my point. Look around and see how many people are divorced, depressed, or living with mental illness; turn on your TV and see all the horrible cases of domestic violence and gun violence. Just go to your local criminal court and see how many child abuse cases, thefts, murders, and other social crimes are committed. I don't have to produce data to prove that we live in a broken world.

If formal education were enough, we would have enough doctors and nurses, and you wouldn't see sick people all over the world. We have enough politicians, administrators, and institutions in the world like the United Nations, that share the goal of eradicating poverty. Still, according to WFP (United Nations World Food Program), *some 795 million people in the world do not have enough food to lead a healthy, active life. That's about one in nine people on earth. The vast majority of the world's hungry people live in developing countries, where 12.9 percent of the population is undernourished—a world where 1/3 of food is wasted.*

Source: https://www.wfp.org/news/world-hunger
-falls-under-800-million-eradication-next-goal-0

This book is not about global poverty, but I think you understand my point of view. I believe it's up to each of us to informally educate ourselves to live fruitfully, happily, and be healthy human beings to heal the world.

I believe the world longs for these people, and you can find them everywhere. Look into your life and see a person who always inspires you and wants to make you strive for more. I bet this person is the kind of person I am talking about.

As an immigrant to a new country, informal education is your best friend. For example, it helps you learn how to interview for a job. It enables you to develop your communication skills and even manage your anger, as discussed in the last chapter.

Now we have established the importance of informal education. Let's see how you can get it.

Reading

Reading is one way to learn. It could be reading books and magazines. Reading has many benefits: It increases your vocabulary and helps you develop your communication skills, just to mention two of many.

I grew up loving to read. When I was a kid, I had a wonderful neighbor, Tibereh, who didn't have children, and she treated me like I was her child.

Tibereh was a Catholic school teacher, and she brought me my first book when I was around seven. I still remember that. It was **Pinocchio**, translated in the Amharic language (Ethiopian National language). Every evening she would read to me and sometimes asked me to read by myself while supervising. She always brought me a new book every time we finished the book we were reading. She was consistent and gentle, so I was hooked on reading for life.

Before I knew it, I read all the fiction books translated into Amharic. I read almost all the books that were available to me at that time. Reading became part of who I am, thanks to Tibereh. Now, every night, before we go to bed, I read a chapter to my sons. I also used to read to my younger sister when she was little, and now she is also an avid reader. My hope is my children will be readers too. Tibereh made such a difference in my life, and I am always grateful to her because she gave me a tool to navigate the big scary world early on.

As immigrants, we have a lot to learn; I am referring to the informal way of learning, as we discussed above. Reading is a fantastic way of learning the skills that we need to acquire. There are many books released daily. There are fiction and nonfiction books on so many topics.

As a kid, I started with fiction books and loved them until I finished high school. Reading fiction is a beautiful way to explore other people, their lives, other countries—and they learn what is essential for other people, about different kinds of personalities and all that. Fiction books helped me see outside of my life and where I lived; they expanded my imagination. I knew some things were possible even though they were not around me.

Books are an excellent way to understand the western world and its dynamics. If you pick fiction for that purpose, I suggest you select drama fiction because it reveals family dynamics and teaches you about the culture. It can also be relaxing and take you away from your situation and routine; possibly, it can feel like going on a vacation. I highly recommend that you choose a book in English or your new country's language, so you can learn the language at the same time you enjoy a story.

Reading is part of my life, and I love it. I love learning and expanding my mind. It's a good habit I developed; thank God for my neighbor who taught me the value of reading. She was indeed my childhood mentor.

I suggest putting money aside to buy books every month. If money is tight, you can find books at a thrift store at a very economical price. You can also borrow books for free at your local library. Getting in the habit of reading will serve you well in your new country. Start at a pace you feel comfortable. Perhaps read a page before going to bed, then increase how much you read every day or night, whatever works for you.

Movies Play the Same Role as Books

When I first came to the US, people told me how surprised they were with my English fluency and that I'd only lived in the USA for a short time. Some people think I was born with a talent for language. They may be right as I agree I might have the innate talent for language, but I also worked hard to master English, and I am still learning every day.

I remember back in Eritrea; I borrowed movies and books from the library every week to practice my English. I remember asking many people the meaning of words I didn't know. I also spent a lot of time referring to a dictionary. Although some people think I have a natural predisposition towards the language, I struggled with English. I was behind my peers in spelling and understanding English when we got to seventh grade, where all the subjects were taught in English. I used to feel so embarrassed to ask my cousin to help me understand this overwhelming foreign language. Luck had nothing to do with it. It was all hard work. I worked hard to read children's books in English, watch movies in English, and make friends with people who spoke only English to practice what I learned.

I love movies and TV shows. I used to joke around and tell people that I speak well because I watch too many American films. All jokes aside, reading and movies helped me perfect my oral English. I love movies because you can hear what the actors say instead of hearing it in your head like when you read books. When watching movies, you hear the correct pronunciation as well.

Besides their benefits as entertainment or tool to learn a particular language, movies are also good storytellers of their culture. Again, watching dramas—but not limiting to that—helps you understand the country's culture, values, norms, hopes, dreams, and fantasies. Most of all, you get to learn some skills that you didn't know. For example, let me share some of the skills I got from TV shows I watched, even though I wasn't looking for them.

From the TV show *Grey's Anatomy*, I learned how I could be a strong career woman and, at the same time, be gentle. From the TV show, *Friends*, I learned a lot about American culture and how friendship works, and many good laughs. From *Gossip Girl*, I watched how rich people interact and learned about their belief system about life, and how it is different from the middle class and low income. By watching the show 13 *Reasons Why*, I learned what kids in high school deal with, which helps when I am talking to high school students. These are just a few to mention.

We make sure our kids watch the cartoon *Super Why* to learn to question things and find solutions in books. Our kids are bombarded with so much technology, and I know I can't avoid that, so my husband and I make sure everything they watch, read, and play with is educational.

Take time in your busy schedule to watch drama movies and TV, but don't be limited to that; always be aware of what you are learning. It could be a word you never heard of before. It could be pronunciation, a social skill, a cultural manner, or it could be all of the above. Make sure you enjoy the movie and the story as well but let it be purposeful!

The USA has an abundance of other opportunities you can choose from to educate yourself. There are classes you can take at a community college or adult school near you. It could be an online course you can enroll in, going to a workshop at your library or school. Utilize them.

Our attitude should always be to keep learning something new because, believe it or not, we will never run out of things to know. Thank God for that, because if we ran out of things to learn, I would die of boredom. There is always something for us to learn, no matter how educated or how much we know.

When you always have that attitude, you will make time in your schedule to learn something new. Some people say learning as an adult takes time. Yes, it may take time, and with patience, consistency, and commitment, you will pass through the pain of learning and be what you want to be. That is a promise! As immigrants, this skill will come in handy in achieving our goals and achieving the American dream.

I previously mentioned that I would talk about the support system in a different chapter. In chapter six, we will take a more in-depth look at how to build your support system from scratch, more about communication, and more on jobs and careers.

CHAPTER 6

SKILLSET #4: BUILDING A SUPPORT SYSTEM FROM SCRATCH

After a few months, the excitement of coming to America and the feeling of accomplishment for making it this far wears off. You have unpacked your things, and you realize something is missing—your support system. And if you are like me, you don't know how you built a support system around you to sustain your emotional life before coming to the USA. It naturally happened through time. I didn't appreciate how easy it was to call a friend after work and get together to have a cappuccino (it's equivalent to getting together for coffee in the US) and talk about what happened during the week. Afterward, I would go home feeling better, and so would my friend, after sharing about her day and week with me. I use to go with friends for a walk around downtown in the beautiful city of Asmara, in Eritrea. Or just

133

come home from work at 5 pm, relax with family around a coffee ceremony (that takes about an hour or two), sit there and talk, have dinner, and relax to watch a movie or TV.

Coming to the US, if you have a family waiting for you here and have a few old friends from back home, then move on; you don't need this chapter. Skip it entirely because you are one of the few lucky ones. But if you are like most of us and you came with no one here, this will be a challenge, but it can be a rewarding journey, so keep reading.

When we were kids and possibly teenagers, we built our support system effortlessly. It's hard to go back to see if the system was created for us or if we chose our support system, other than our family, of course.

We may have had friends that we met in kindergarten, primary school, high school, or even university or college. And it came naturally because those were friends that were probably the same age, studied the same subjects, and lived in the same city.

As you go from one educational institution to another, you keep the friends you like and connected with, and you continued getting together even though you no longer go to the same school. You make an effort to stay in touch, but some friendships naturally fall out as you move forward with your life. And this is very normal for everyone.

Some special friendships withstand the distance and the lack of contact for many years; and, once rekindled through Facebook or phone, they spark again. I don't know why some friendships from the past flourish when the opportunity presents itself and some friendships don't survive. Sometimes there's too much of a gap, and they automatically wither away, which is also standard and accepted.

After your international move and many phone calls, you may begin to understand that the people you left behind have no idea what you are going through. As much as they want to support you, they can't understand and relate to your circumstances because it's hard for them to imagine what it's like for you in your new country. With this discovery, you may start feeling frustrated.

No matter how close you may feel, old relationships might start to feel strange, and your calls may drop off. If this happens, it is ok. It's because you need a different support system for your new experience. It doesn't mean you need to discard the old friendships; they might rekindle someday when the time comes. It's worth maintaining them by calling once in a while or staying connected through social media, looking at each other's lives growing in different directions. However, your friends back home are not actually with you for this part of your adventurous life.

When you realize your old friendships will not support your emotional needs anymore, you may feel frustration, loneliness, depression, and anger.

At some point, you realize you have to rebuild new friendships from scratch—which is typically a long process. It can feel daunting to start this process again, even if you feel you urgently need a support system for your current situation. It takes time. So be patient.

Every time you face a challenge, you feel the lack of support weighing on you, which may make you feel more frustrated and angry.

You may realize you didn't appreciate what you had till you lost it, and may grieve the loss of what was familiar, your friends and all of it. You may realize you even start to miss the people that used to annoy you!

Making new friends in your new country becomes like a vast mountain to climb, and you feel anxious. It's even worse if you are an introvert person and you only had a few friends to begin with.

Some people who have gone through the same process may tell you, "You'll be fine once you get into the system," "Everything will be okay. You will get busy, get a job, and it will all work out." Or they may say, "Keep doing what you're doing; it will make sense later."

In my case, that kind of advice didn't help me at all because it didn't show me how to overcome my anger and frustrations when I didn't know how to do something. When I couldn't understand what I was doing or where I was going; and whenever I lost sight of the "big picture" and almost felt like giving up and going back home. It's important to get the "how-to," the steps explained, and not just advice like "you're going to make it."

However, when people tell you, "Don't worry, you're going to make it" or "You will be okay," Don't take it personally. Maybe they have forgotten their experiences or are so busy and don't have time to empathize with what you're going through. It's easier for them to say you'll be fine. Trust me, most people who tell you these things sincerely and emotionally want to help you, even if what they say is not helpful at all.

It may feel like they're ignoring you, or being dismissive, or trying to minimize what you're going through. Don't go there. Get up right now and tell your mind that's not the case. It's not true. Self-pity doesn't work for anyone. We all go through these feelings, and we overcome them. You are not alone; let this be the voice of sanity. Don't go down the negative path, the road of isolating yourself from everyone.

You may also meet people who have been in the US for more than ten, even twenty, years that are still stuck on that road. They think they know what cultural integration is, that there is no more than this, and advise to follow the same path. Their path, however, paints the American dream as nothing but a dream that you can't reach. The urge to associate with friends who think like this is hard to fight off. Their friendship might feel like something you have been looking for. After all, it seems that someone has understood what you have been experiencing and feeling. I can totally relate, you are right. And it might even be possible to build a great friendship just by talking about all the negative aspects of your American experience. However, it would be an unhealthy friendship, and may only feel good temporarily.

Although you may have found a place to dump your frustration, it is a toxic relationship that will keep you drained and stuck in the same place without progress down the road, and it may be hard to break free.

I will say more about toxic relationships later. For now, I want you to understand that this road isn't the right road to go on because it will not benefit your well-being or cultural integration, and will create more problems along the way. It will prevent you from integrating into the culture successfully. Also, it will distort your vision of America.

Now, we have looked at some of the roads that are available to you and, without guidance, you might, not know how to get what you want, which is to meet people, make great connections, create meaningful friendships, and maintain them.

Where do you start? The road to this future is even more frustrating because there is no map you can follow since very few defined the way. You might hear about some people, but you don't know how to get to them. It becomes a myth to you, and you feel like it isn't possible, and you feel anxious and frustrated all the time.

I get it. And if you are reading this book and you are in this process, don't fret, take a deep breath because this book is your road map. I will not walk the walk for you, but I can show you where the mental road lies and what you will find on the road, so you can walk it with confidence.

Start by making a list: if you somehow know you have old friends in the US, try to connect with them. Nowadays, tools like Facebook increase the chance of connecting with old friends by merely searching their names; if that doesn't work, you could reach out to all the friends you have in all states and see if friendships rekindle.

I have to warn you; not all friendships will rekindle; in fact, most friendships you had wouldn't be the same; this is normal, as we all potentially grow apart, not having anything in common anymore. Don't get discouraged; you only need one or two friends from your past for your initial support system. Keep calling and give all of them a chance. I often hear people giving up after a few tries and say, "it's hard to be friends again after being separated for a long time." That is simply not true.

Once you have found one or two friends you feel good reconnecting with that you can talk to regularly, even if it is over the phone, the next step will be for you to expand your support system. From my experience, having one friend or a family member who is like a friend is really important but not enough. You have many emotional/spiritual needs, and expecting one person to fulfill all your needs is too much pressure for the friendship, and you might risk breaking the friendship if you don't handle it carefully. Now that we agree that you need to expand your support system, let's explore the attitude, tools, and skills required to develop a support system that sustains and fulfills you.

The first step: Check your mental attitude toward this process.

Mental Attitude

When I talk to many, including very close friends, and my clients, I hear, "We're too old to make new friends now. New friends are not going to be like the old friends that we made a long time ago. It's just impossible to make friends that understand me in this culture."

You are right! But not in the way you may think. Your concerns may be right for you because you believe it is true, so no one has a chance to be friends with you because you are always looking at the potential friend with this attitude. The friendship will not develop mainly because of your belief.

Suppose you are holding your fist in front of your chest and closing off your heart with a mental belief that is not true. In this case, you will never make any real new connections, and if you do make new connections, they won't turn into a fulfilling relationship because you have a standard that isn't realistic.

The friends you make now are not going to be like friends from your childhood or younger years. Your new friends are there to walk with you in your current living situation. Your friends from primary school weren't the same as the friends you made in high school, and friends you made in college weren't the same as your high school friends. The friends you make in the US will be different from those you made in the past. So make peace with that.

I had an Eritrean friend who at some point moved to Oregon from California. After three years, we called each other, and I asked her how she was and about her new friends. She laughed and said, "Oh my God, Senait, every time you ask me that, I laugh. I think making friends is so easy for you, and you assume it should be easy for everyone else." She said she had not made a single friend in three years!

Her response came as a shock because I never thought that my natural tendency to connect with people was considered a skill. For confirmation, I asked people close to me if they believed that way too. I checked with all my friends and family, and they confirmed the same. One family member said to me, jokingly, "You know you can talk to a stone if you need to." It was so surprising to me to find out about a skill I developed, which I thought came naturally to everyone. I sincerely thought everybody possessed this gift.

Ever since I was a kid, I struggled with having friends. I made connections with people right away, and people always surrounded me, but I struggled to navigate my friendships and maintain them. More than anything, I wanted to create meaningful friendships, and I realized this skill and now have friendships in my life I cherish.

However, I was not aware I had been working toward that goal unconsciously. I meditated on this for a while, and I realized I had developed a skill to maintain relationships. I realized that my life was full of tried and true friendships that went deep. I also have friends with connections not as deep, but still significant and more profound over time, as we gain more experience together. Believe it or not, I made most of my vital relationships after I moved to the USA.

I was really in awe of this realization, and I am writing about some of the tools that got me where I am today, so you can also enjoy abundance in the area of friendships and emotional support if you struggle in this area.

If you learn anything from reflecting on your attitude, please let it change your mind about not making friends after a certain age. It's only right as much as you want to make it. Holding this belief, we miss the opportunity that turns strangers into our spouses, to our best friends, a great neighbor, and finally, a family by choice. You will be missing out on a lot just by tightly holding on to that false belief. So, let it go and be open to people.

Boundaries

This tool is my favorite one. Like I told you before, I don't know how but I have always been good at talking to strangers and making a real connection at any moment. I also shared earlier that my biggest struggle was keeping meaningful friendships. I had seen all kinds of friends, ones that only hung around with me when they needed something, and some that worked hard to isolate me from every other friendship I had. I have been with friends that were too demanding and accused me of not being available to their needs. I was not accessible enough. Even though I found it easy to make connections and new friends, I was puzzled by the nature of the friendships or how to maintain them. Which mostly left me feeling used, unappreciated, and confused.

It took me years before I found the missing piece to my problem. Boundaries! I didn't understand the definition until eleven years ago. I was born in a culture where boundaries are fuzzy or nonexistent.

I never had my room growing up as I shared a bed with my brother and sister when we were young. Traditionally, we all ate from the same plate. As kids, when we went outside to play with many other kids in the neighborhood, if I did something wrong, my friend's mom had the right to discipline me, even physically, as this was customary. To sum it up, although I was born to my parents, I was everybody's business. (I really understand and lived the African proverb, "It takes a village to raise a child.") Everybody in my neighborhood raised me. There was no sense of me, I, or my. It was always we.

142

Physical boundaries were nonexistent. Growing up and making friends, I complained about people all the time. Such as, someone did this or that to me, or someone dared to say that to me. The persistent complaining followed me in my adult life.

My friend, Grandma Sue, may God rest her soul, who I met right after I moved to the US, listened to me many times and told me that I needed to strengthen my boundaries. At first, I wondered, "What does she mean? What is she talking about? What do boundaries have to do with anything?" It took me over six months to understand the concept. Yep! That was one of the most significant discoveries of my adult life, and it has changed my whole relationship experience.

I read every book on boundaries and codependency, and my relationships transformed like day and night. I finally was able to seek out only healthy friendships and relationships and transform those that were unhealthy, if I couldn't let go. Of course, I got rid of many friendships that weren't healthy for me, nor the other person.

I am telling you this tool is my favorite. So what are boundaries? The dictionary defines "boundary" as a line that marks an area's limits, a dividing line. I came from a region where there are continuous border conflicts. I am aware of this line, and it's easy to understand it on a piece of land. So how is this going to help me find healthy friendships and keep them? I learned over the years that there are different types of boundaries. Physical, Emotional, Sexual, Intellectual, Material, and Time are some of the most important ones. I will touch all of them here, but the discussion's focus will be mostly on physical and emotional boundaries.

1. Physical

Physical boundaries include personal space and physical touch. Ladies, has anyone ever rummaged through your purse without asking?

Has anyone hugged you after just meeting them? Does either of these examples make you squirm? That reactivity is your body telling you it's a physical boundary; whether it's your personal body space or your personal environment, it has been violated. You may welcome a hug from a long-time friend over a stranger on the street, just as you may be more comfortable allowing your daughter to grab your phone out of your purse than you might be with a passerby in the store. Healthy physical boundaries include an awareness of what's appropriate in varying settings and relationships.

2. Emotional

Emotional boundaries refer to our feelings, including our expressiveness. These can be violated when we are criticized or invalidated. Has anyone ever said to you, "there's no reason to be upset" or "you're making a big deal out of nothing?" Even if they're trying to console you, this can feel damaging and leave us feeling unheard and dismissed. Healthy emotional boundaries include personal limitations we set for sharing personal information.

3. Intellectual

Intellectual boundaries are slightly less obvious yet likely happen more often than we think. Intellectual boundaries refer to our thoughts and ideas and are repeatedly violated when someone dismisses or belittles them. Have you ever had an idea you were excited about and shared with someone and was quickly shut down? Afterward, you may feel like you want to hide in a hole for weeks. Or you shared insight on a political topic (who hasn't these days?), and someone from an opposing party berated you. It happens all the time. Healthy intellectual boundaries will include respectfulness and a willingness to understand not only one's ideas and values but others as well, even if they are opposing our own.

4. Sexual

Sexual boundaries compile the physical, emotional, and intellectual aspects of sexuality. What does this mean? Essentially, any unwanted sexual touch, ogling from others, sexual comments, or pressure to engage in sexual acts can qualify as a destruction of a sexual boundary. Curious about what the #MeToo movement represents? That's it, folks—violated sexual boundaries. Healthy sexual boundaries will include consent, mutual agreement, respect, and understanding of the limits and desires discussed between intimate or sexual partners.

5. Material

Material boundaries refer to personal possessions. Does someone you know always ask to borrow money but never pay you back? Or maybe you lent your friend an iPad, and they returned it broken? When someone pressures you to give or lend them your possessions or steals, damages, or destroys your possessions, the boundary has likely been violated. Healthy material boundaries include limitations on what you choose to share and with whom.

6. Time

Time boundaries reference how we use our time. These boundaries are a bit trickier to notice but are very apparent all the same. They are often violated when someone demands too much of another's time. Do you find yourself always setting aside your plans because a friend continually wants to hang out instead? Or maybe your partner gives you grief for trying to take time for yourself or hang out with friends? You can implement healthy time boundaries by setting aside time for your lives' various facets, including work, hobbies, and relationships, considering your values and priorities.

Source: https://www.thepracticeatx.com/mental-health -blog/2017/11/14/six-boundaries-that-can-change-your-life

Ok, now we understand what a boundary is; how do we set up and enforce our boundaries? It is an entirely different thing because you got to learn the hardest thing in the world: to say "No." And telling people what you like and you don't like.

I see my 2½-year-old son saying "NO" to everything we say to him. I smile and wonder when do we, as adults, lose our no's. It took me many years of suffering to learn to say no appropriately to people close to me. Somehow in my mind, I thought saying no to my family and friends meant being rude. Rude=No. Ha! I found out how wrong that long-held belief was and the price I paid along the way.

My son does it so naturally. We are born naturally to say no to things we don't want or to something that we don't like. If I give my son a banana, he says no and sometimes asks for an apple. I say, "Let's go to the park," and he says no. He wants to watch a movie instead. He is still discovering his boundaries and sometimes gets very upset when we say no to things we don't allow him because it endangers his safety or doesn't go with our family values. In those moments, he's discovering his limits, and he would eventually accept someone saying no to him and would learn the consequence of crossing our boundaries. My husband and I know how to keep saying no to him and enforce our boundaries.

Yes, boundaries are great tools for everyone in our lives. If you want to be healthy emotionally, intellectually and maintain healthy relationships and friendships, you must learn to set your boundaries with everyone in your life.

Yes, even with your husband, wife, kids (especially your kids). As well as your best friends, your parents, your boss, social workers—no exceptions.

I won't lie to you; setting boundaries is one of the most challenging things you do, but the most rewarding. Especially if you didn't grow up with boundary-setting skills, prepare yourself for the challenge. There will be some hiccups, some trial and error, and you might anger some people close to you who are accustomed to a certain availability. You might even lose some friendships that wouldn't survive this boundary-setting process. I promise you will be fine! You don't want to be with people who continuously cross your boundary and make you feel disrespected.

You need to know that a boundary is a personal thing; no two people have the same limitations, and we all have the personal power to set our boundaries as we see fit. You don't need someone else's approval to set your boundaries.

The hardest thing for me when I was identifying my boundaries was that I didn't know where my limits were. So how could I set them when I didn't know what they were? It was tricky, but after trying many things, I finally realized that whenever I felt angry, distressed, uncomfortable, it was an indication pointing me to where my boundaries were. So I started to look at what made me angry or frustrated about what someone said or did, and I discovered those were the moments that they had crossed my boundaries. Once I realized it, I started setting my boundaries.

So now, take a look at your life and your relationships and identify where you feel angry, frustrated, sad, helpless with someone. See if you can find where your boundaries are. That is Step 1.

Step 2. Tell people in your life what you are up to and what they should expect from you. Since I started to set boundaries, I have learned a lot; back then, I was so excited and eager to live a healthy emotional life that I placed my boundaries with everyone around me forcefully and with passion. I remember I faced a lot of resistance; close family members got so mad at me.

Don't get afraid or alarmed; it's part of the process. Most people in your life will come around and respect your boundaries, and you will renew your friendships, but it takes consistency and time.

Some will fall off; those are people you are better off without because they refuse to respect who you are and who you are becoming. If I could go back and do it differently, I would have followed Step 2, as I do now whenever I set my boundary and enforce them. Yes, boundaries evolve when your life evolves, so this is an ongoing process.

Whenever you find a new boundary, acknowledge it, and then have a conversation with your family or friends. Tell them about that particular incident that bothered you and how you found out. Let them know that you will speak up politely to remind them of boundaries crossed. It works like a charm when an opportunity comes up to enforce it. You could say, "I don't like it when you do that." Then they would think, "Oh, that's what she/he was talking about the other day," and they will be mindful of your boundaries.

Telling people you interact with to stop a behavior that has been considered normal without explaining yourself may come off as rude.

Always tell people closest to you what you are trying to achieve, that you are going to set your boundaries. It will only make it easier for you and them. We are complex creatures, and if you find a limit that is causing you to be upset with someone, tell them.

When a boundary you weren't previously aware of surprises you, and you react by shouting at someone with anger, come back after you cool off, apologize, and explain what happened. You may want to say, "I am sorry I shouted at you earlier, but I just found a new boundary for myself, and I need to take time to understand it. I will talk to you again about it." It will automatically give you a peaceful break from people. You can come back later and say, "I am so sorry I reacted that way with you the other day. I apologize that I hurt your feelings; however, I discovered that I don't like it when people do this (whatever the violation was). Would you please not do that?" Boom! That gives you power over your boundaries without losing your unique connection with your family or friends.

Consistency/Enforcement

Step 3 is very crucial. It's the hardest part of all and yet the most important, because without this step you have nothing. You may have identified your current boundaries, and you may have many more to add in the future; however, it's nothing without enforcement and without being consistent.

People will test your boundaries to see if you are serious. They though you talked about them. Some people may resist and purposely want to cross your boundaries, even if they're close relatives or have known you for a long time.

Some people may have a passive-aggressive attitude, pretending they forgot, pretending not to pay attention, or intentionally continuing to cross your boundaries. You may have many challenges and resistances along the way, and the only way to go through this stage is to enforce your new boundaries consistently.

I enjoy teaching my little son Joseph about boundaries. He resists some of the limitations we have put in place, like not playing with garbage or not hitting people. When his dad and I consistently enforce those boundaries, Joseph can get upset. He doesn't like it and wants to keep testing our boundaries. He might cry or throw things at us. We have to admit this isn't our favorite part of parenting, but we also know that at some point, he will start respecting the boundaries and structures we have set for him. We might have to endure several tantrums, headbangs, and lots and lots of crying, but we must consistently enforce the boundaries. We know it might take time before he gets it. Until then, every time Joseph goes to the garbage bin and opens it, if we see him, we say firmly, "Joseph! NO! We don't put our hands in the garbage bin, and we don't play with garbage."

Kids test our boundaries, and as adults, when faced with something new that disrupts our routine life, it's normal to feel resistance to it. It's inconvenient and, like when we were babies, we act with frustration, anger, sadness, and depression in extreme cases.

When you try to enforce your boundaries, people will resist. Expect it, be patient. But most importantly, no matter how much you love them, don't just think, "It's ok, I already talked to them, maybe they forgot, and they will get it next time." When people cross your boundaries, let them know right away. Don't ignore it. It will not work. I have walked this path before; it will only lead to one destination. Both you and the person you are setting a boundary with are feeling frustrated and angry at each other. Please, I know this will feel uncomfortable, but there is no way around it. After you follow Step 2 and talk to the person, watch your own behavior like a soldier. Often, it's your reaction, not the other person's, that causes tension. The next time the person crosses your boundaries, you will see you feel angry, irritated, or frustrated. When you sense that, take a deep breath, and you can say to the person, "Wait, let's take a moment here, I feel angry/irritated (whatever you are feeling), and I know it's because you are crossing my boundary. I don't like it when you do this. Could you please not do it again? Thank you." Say this as many times as you need to until your boundary is respected.

Ideally, the other person will understand immediately. It could happen rarely if you are dealing with an emotionally evolved person. However, I have yet to meet that person. Mostly, you will get a reaction; some people will rudely react because they feel embarrassed. When confronted, some will respond in frustration, and most people will get defensive. People will respond in all kinds of ways.

Your challenge here is to calmly hold your ground because that might trigger your anger as well. Know and understand, the person you are dealing with is trying to sort out your new boundary in the way he/she knows how. Be patient, and you can say, "I am sorry. I don't mean to make you feel angry, defensive, or frustrated. I don't like it when people do this or that. It makes me feel angry and irritated, and I will keep reminding you about that till it doesn't happen again."

For the rest of your life, keep using the tools to discover new boundaries; your life changes and grows, and once you find a new boundary, set it and be consistent. If there are people who refuse to respect your boundaries, be willing to let them go. You can't be in a relationship if you are continually feeling upset and frustrated. It's not worth it. Letting them go and ending the relationship may be right for both of you in the long run.

Perhaps there is a family relationship you can't get rid of, like a friendship. All you can do in that case is:

- Limit the amount of time you spend with them
- Always remind them when your boundaries are crossed
- Love them from a distance

Getting Your Needs Met/Communication

Most of us grew up conditioned not to ask for what we want. Different cultures may have various reasons for conditioning their community, but no one taught me how to ask for what I want. I see children, including mine, using different methods to get their needs met.

Every parent knows that babies communicate with us from birth. They will cry and cry for everything they need. We have to find out why they are crying; is it because they are hungry, wet, sick, or need comfort? Babies slowly learn to communicate with words. Somewhere in the process, they know they're not getting everything they want, so it's easy to start using different tactics like manipulation, aggression, or being sweet to get their needs met. It's smart and ok for babies to do that.

However, as an adult, we continue to do the same thing, even as the different experiences in our lives contribute to our belief that we can't always get what we want. We develop some wrong beliefs that we are not worthy, that we are not enough, that it's not ok to focus on what we need. Some cultures shame people for asking for what they want. The belief that if I ask for what I need, I will be considered selfish.

Other circumstances may cause you not to say what you want. It might be that you don't feel safe to ask for what you need because the person you are requesting something from to scares you and is violent.

During our early adult life experience, many things happen to us that make us think we can't ask for what we want, which becomes a belief. So we continue this unhealthy behavior, which brings a lot of disruption and dysfunction in our family and communities, and, on a larger scale, the world.

This topic is so vast I could write a book dedicated to it. However, below are a few tips to help you get your needs met.

The first thing we will do is take a commonsense approach to change your belief. You will need to make peace with the fact that you will not get what you want all the time, no matter who you are.

This awareness alone is enough to snap us out of the need to manipulate others.

The next one is another commonsense fact that we know, but we often don't realize that you deserve to get your needs met. Of course! Why wouldn't you, unless it's harmful to you? If you are also a parent, you know that we would try and do everything in our power to get our kids' needs met as much as our finances and abilities allow. If your child comes to you and says, "I don't deserve to have that," you will break into tears. You are there to provide, and your kids think they can't have their needs met? I would get upset, too; why would we believe we don't deserve something we want? So drop the belief. You deserve every good thing in this world. Everybody's needs are different; my needs are different from yours. Whatever they are, though, you deserve it, and you can get your needs met.

I had a conversation with a friend of mine once; she told me that she loves diamonds and it makes her happy to buy them. She also said she loves BMW cars and bought one. I sensed in her voice that she was feeling guilty. It sounded like she was trying to convince me, and herself, of the legitimate reasons she loves those things. I said to her, "Why are you explaining that to me? You buy what you need to feel happy. It's your money; you worked hard for it, and if you want to spend it on jewelry and luxury cars, go for it. I am happy for you." She felt relieved. Most of us go around feeling guilty for getting the things we love with our money. What is that, but our social conditioning and our personal belief system?

Women are typically more afraid than men to ask for what they want, but some men are also afraid to ask for what they want in their relationships and friendships. This kind of fear leads us to believe that we don't deserve what we want.

Some use unhealthy ways to get what we want. Let's see some unhealthy behaviors that you might even recognize in your own family and friends circle.

Manipulation

Manipulators try to get you to do something that you might not want to do by using different techniques, like making you feel guilty or by dropping suggestions and messing with your mind.

When I first moved to the US, I had a close friend: I will call her Stacy for privacy purposes. She was a manipulator.

I could never figure out whether she was afraid that I would say "no" if she just simply asked for what she wanted. I tried to assure her that it was okay to ask but no matter what I tried, the manipulative behavior or what she wanted but, no matter what I tried, the behavior continued, and that relationship didn't survive.

It doesn't feel right when people manipulate you to get their needs met, it feels icky. I remember one day I told Stacy something personal that I lived to regret. She used the information I shared to her advantage instead of asking me directly what she needed from me, like accompanying her to someplace where she didn't want to go alone. Stacy would bring up the personal matter I shared with her as a threat, reminding me that my secret wasn't safe with her. It was crazy. I eventually told our mutual friends my secret to break free from Stacy's manipulation then I ended our toxic relationship as it made my life less enjoyable.

If you have friends like Stacy, don't tolerate their behavior. By accepting toxic behaviors, we allow them to continue to exist. Confront the person who is doing it. Assure them they don't have to do that with you and that it's okay for them to ask you directly. If they keep doing it and their behavior upsets you, ending the relationship might be your best bet. Ending relationships may feel rude and inhuman; however, your goal is to surround yourself with mentally and emotionally healthy people willing to work on themselves as much as you do to support one another to achieve your goals and dreams.

You don't need people who drag you back and cause a lot of stress in your life. You have no time for that. When I ended my relationship with Stacy, I had a hard time. I had to consult a counselor to help with the best way to end the relationship. No matter what I did, the best way was to be direct and tell the truth. By being straightforward and truthful, you allow others to do the same.

I told Stacy I loved her and shared all I learned from her, such as the positive qualities I loved and admired about her, which were all true. I also shared with Stacy that, at that time in my life, I needed to be around people that could support and sustain me as much as I would help them and that her behavior wasn't something I could handle. I was sorry, but I had to let the relationship go.

My friend said, "Okay, of course." She was offended and kept practicing her manipulative behavior. I had to say goodbye and left. I could have ended the relationship by disappearing or avoiding her, but that wouldn't help Stacy learn from the experience. It would have deprived me of practicing my assertive skills. Truth hurts, but that is always the way to go.

Shaming and Aggression

Some people use shame and aggression to get what they want. Similar to manipulation, but this one is more forceful.

Recently, I saw someone I had known for a while; we will call him Bill; we've always been friendly. However, I noticed he wasn't as pleasant as usual. Instantly, I figured I had done something wrong. Soon, he broke into aggression, shaming me and explaining what a bad friend I had been to him and that he didn't deserve the way I treated him.

I was puzzled. What was going on? I tried to find out what was happening and found out he was upset because I came back without seeing his brother when I visited Eritrea after 11 years. I told him I went there only for a week and he didn't ask me to see his brother whom I didn't even know, by the way.

I have heard him say many times before my visit that his brother actually travels a lot, and I didn't even know he was in Eritrea when I was there. I tried to explain how my time there was not enough to see my family, but he didn't want to hear it. He left upset, telling me how good he has been to me and how dare I go back and not see his brother.

Unfortunately, I see this kind of behavior a lot. It's an expectation that's not communicated. How do I know unless you ask me what you want? How do I know if it's important to you unless you tell me directly? We expect things from others without them being aware. When we have unrealistic expectations of others, we get upset, leaving the other person very confused.

Especially in a romantic relationship, this could be detrimental. I've heard men complain about this, and I have coached women who shared with me how upset they were because their partner failed them. When I pointed out that they never communicated that with the partner, they would get more upset and say, "It's obvious, he is supposed to know!"

How should he know?

Now, we have an upset wife for her lack of communication and a husband who is left confused and feeling resentful. The wife would go on for days shaming and being aggressive to the husband, but that aggression and shaming don't get her what she wants; it just gets more misunderstanding and resentment in the relationship.

These are just a few unhealthy ways we try to communicate what we want and need. Other toxic behaviors destroy friendships and relationships, so be aware of those in your actions and correct them; watch for those behaviors in people you know and try to avoid them unless you want to get their toxicity in your life. Focus on your goals and dreams, do not get tangled or trapped up in a drama of other people.

Other Toxic Behaviors

People who like to gossip and enjoy drama. Those people love to talk about other people and not in a friendly way. Know that those people are addicted to gossip, and therefore they might go somewhere else and talk about you behind your back.

Even if you offer help and solutions, they never seem to want to fix anything. Instead, they complain and complain.

It never stops; they complain about their lives and other people. They gossip and put others down. And as much as you want to help them, you can't. These kinds of people need professional help. Trying to fix their problem will only depress you.

If you put some toxic substance into clean water, it will soon be undrinkable, and hanging out with some toxic people can ruin your life. It doesn't mean we as humans don't complain; some amount of complaining is ok, so don't dismiss anyone who might complain, but look for excessive repetition of this behavior in someone who is a chronic complainer and doesn't want to change his/her life.

I learned this in my university years with a friend I had; we will call her Winta. She was always talking about other people and complaining about everything and everyone. I usually asked her, "How do you know? Not everybody is bad; it's good to see the positive in others instead of focusing only on the negative." I thought it was my responsibility to be a good friend by trying to fix the behavior.

I didn't notice at first how many friends started avoiding me. Finally, I learned that Winta, who had become like family to me rather than just a friend, had been spreading gossip about me among familiar

160

friends and acquaintances. The day I heard this, I refused to believe the person who told me. I thought they were jealous of my friendship with Winta and wanted to get in between us. However, when a second person, then a third, confirmed what the first person told me, I was left feeling vulnerable, angry, and betrayed. I ended the relationship after confronting her.

Now looking back, I realize that my friend has been the same person from day one. When she talked about other people and complained about everything and everyone, it should have been my clue to stay away from this person, because she will do and say things about me. I didn't know what I know now. I didn't recognize that friendship was toxic.

Sometimes avoiding gossip might be challenging. In a work environment or among your friends, gossip might be typical. And you might feel like not participating prevent you from fitting in. However, put a boundary in the beginning when it happens and make it clear that you don't like or want to talk about other people behind their backs; continue to enforce your boundaries. People might not understand initially but will start to respect you for your stand and come around. Yes, this will require you to be brave, but in the end, you will enjoy a very peaceful life free of all the toxicity that comes from gossip and drama.

The Jealous Type

There are people always jealous of others' achievements and critical of other people. They criticize what you wear, when you put on weight, and try to control your friendship by acting out and telling you bad things about your friends' friends; they want you to hang out with them only. They will try to isolate you. Some people confuse this with love. Please understand: if a person isolates you from others and tells you it's because they love you, don't believe them. It's a very unhealthy behavior and toxic.

We need to take responsibility for our way of communication and unreasonable expectations.

In my experience, what most jealous people want is to be recognized, heard, loved, and to feel important. And since they don't know how to ask for it or get it, they continue this vicious, toxic behavior to get what they want, in a way that is harmful to others.

I could list many more toxic behaviors; however, I want you to look at your relationships to see if they are unhealthy. Here are some common feelings you might have if you are around toxic people:

- You feel like you have to save this person and fix their problems continually
- You are covering up or hiding from them
- You dread seeing them
- You feel drained after being with them
- You get angry, sad, or depressed when you are around them
- You feel forced to talk about others
- You're affected by their drama or problems
- They ignore your needs and don't hear 'no'

If you continuously feel one or more of those feelings when you are around toxic people, say no to that relationship. Walk away before it's too late. You are not wrong for doing it. The guilt you may feel when you get rid of some toxic friendships and relationships is because most of us never learned how a healthy friendship or relationship feels. We didn't have others to model it for us, so most of us have accepted toxic people as something normal.

I see many cases in court where people are going through a very nasty divorce. They are usually very bitter, resentful, and out of control because they have tolerated a toxic behavior for far too long. Their lives have become so poisonous, they can't even think clearly, and they often appear rude even to their lawyers, judges, and the interpreter trying to help them.

I have also come across an attempted murder case where a husband testified he's been tolerating his wife's toxic behavior for far too long, more than ten years. His excuse was that he had to be patient with her for the sake of his children; therefore, he tried to fix his jealous, drama loving, and insecure wife as much as he could. Obviously, he couldn't fix her. Instead, his life had gotten bitter, and he was resentful and angry. One day, he lost his patience and tolerance level and tried to kill her. Luckily for the wife and the kids, she didn't die; you can find this young man behind bars in a United States prison convicted for life.

Toxic behaviors are in marriages and friendships, and found between co-workers, neighbors, etc. I know the situation with the young man who tried to kill his wife is an extreme example. Still, it shows you the potential magnitude of the consequences of tolerating behaviors that we shouldn't accept, which might jeopardize our lives.

A woman from Vietnam, who I was coaching, said, while talking about toxic behavior. "But being patient is a virtue. Maybe if I become more patient and say nothing, he will stop mistreating me knowing that he has done bad."

I have heard this from many people, men and women from different countries. In my culture, this belief is also adopted. However, saying nothing when being mistreated isn't noble. You must define boundaries, and let people know they can't treat you that way and strive for a healthy relationship.

A healthy relationship meets us with our desires and needs. How does it feel? Most of us have dealt with too many toxic families, friendships, and relationships; we don't even know how healthy relationships are supposed to look or feel.

So, let's look at some characteristics of a healthy relationship:

- You feel comfortable being as you are
- You don't have to pretend to be somebody else
- You don't feel rushed or pressured to do what you don't want to do
- There is mutual respect
- There is mutual support
- There is mutual trust: You don't always wonder what the person is going to do next or if they will hurt you. You know for sure they have your back as you have theirs

- You both feel free to have other interests and friends outside of the friendship, relationship, and even marriage without feeling guilty
- You both put equal effort into giving support and maintaining the relationship
- When conflict arises, there is healthy communication to resolve the difference. You talk about it and forgive each other and move on with mutual understanding
- You feel loved, and you express love freely

There are more ways to tell if your relationships and friendships are healthy, but these are common.

Although there are other contributing factors like low self-worth and not feeling loved, most of the dysfunctions and toxic behaviors also come from our failure to communicate what we want and what we need directly.

When we fail to communicate what we want directly and honestly, manipulation, aggressiveness, and scorekeeping become our only attempt to communicate what we want. However, this builds resentment, anger, and distrust that destroy relationships.

In a healthy relationship and friendship, there is honesty, authenticity, and respect for others. We have to learn and master a powerful way of communication.

Let's look at some tips on how we can communicate with others to meet our needs. It's quite simple.

All you have to do is: Identify your needs and what you want and ask for them directly. Know that sometimes you will get a yes, and sometimes you will get a no, and be ok with that. Simple right? But most of us don't tell others what we want because of fear of rejection. We fear upsetting the other person, and we might have different reasons as well. However, our commitment should be toward being a healthy human being and having healthy friendships and relationships. These friendships and relationships should nurture us to grow into our dreams and goals, like trees that get sunshine and water and grow tall and beautiful. Our commitment shouldn't be to our fears.

It's ok to say no to people, and it's ok for others to say no to us. Make peace with it. We don't always get 100% of what we want in life, and that is ok.

Mr. Tafese, my 7th-grade math teacher, used to tell us to study and work hard, always expecting 100%! And when you do, sometimes you might get 100%, and sometimes you might get 90%, which would still be ok. But if you study only to get 50% to pass the exam, you might sometimes get 50% and pass, but sometimes, you might get 40% and fail. So always play to win 100%. Always try hard in everything to get 100%, including when asking for what you want. And if you get 90% of what you asked for, it's still pretty cool!

Unless we learn to communicate our needs honestly and directly, we can't be in a healthy relationship with our family and friends or anyone for that matter. And not mastering this tool becomes an obstacle when we try to build our healthy support system that can nurture our lives.

Let's look at some more examples of how not being assertive about what we want can lead to losing the support and love that we deserve and need.

One of my clients, Mrs. P., had a baby a few years ago. She is from my hometown back in Africa. In Africa, it's a tradition that women who give birth are to rest for 40 days and sometimes longer while eating healthy food prepared by their family. My friend moved to the US after having the baby, and the only family here was her husband.

Mrs. P.'s always-busy husband announced he wanted a guest to come and visit. Although weak from childbirth, she felt obligated to get up and make food for the guest. The guest, who is also from the same hometown, enjoyed the meal prepared by Mrs. P. She never offered to help, while my friend did the dishes, made tea, and entertained her. Even though the lady was a guest, Mrs. P. expected her to have some sensibility since she didn't have anyone else to cook, do dishes, and do the chores. She should have offered help, allowing the new mom to rest, as that is the cultural expectation.

Mrs. P. was upset; she was going on and on telling me how she was so mad on that occasion. I asked her, "Why is it that you wanted and needed at that time?"

Mrs. P. felt irritated by the question. She just wanted me to agree with her that her guest was wrong. I told her that I understood what she wanted from me, but I also wanted to know what she wanted from her guest on that occasion. Mrs. P. said, "I felt weak, tired, and wanted to rest. Although I appreciated the visit, I wanted her to be more empathetic, knowing that I had given birth and didn't have anyone to help out." She continued, "I felt my guest should have helped by cooking, washing dishes, and allowing me to rest. That is what I would have done for someone else."

So, I said to Mrs. P., "Great, so you knew what you wanted and needed at the moment. Yes, she could have been more emphatic about how you were feeling, and she might not be the best guest, and she may have acted selfishly; however, did you communicate that to your guest? Did you show her how tired and weak you were? Or, did you pretend, smile, and looked healthy?"

Mrs. P. admitted she was trying to be strong, wanted to be welcoming, and pretended to smile, so her guest didn't feel bad.

I asked her, what if you said, "I am so happy you came to see me. Thank you! However, I am sorry, but I am tired and feel weak. Normally I would cook and entertain you, but I need to rest more, and I don't have any help, so please forgive me. Please help yourself to make anything you would like. I have everything you need in the kitchen, and if you are not hungry, I also have some milk, juice, or water, and you could help yourself out."

Mrs. P. gasped and said, "Are you crazy? I can't say that!" "Why not?" I asked.

"It's not culturally appropriate for me to treat my guest like that. After all, she came to my house. Secondly, the guest is supposed to know I needed help, it was obvious, and she should have offered to help without me asking. I shouldn't have to ask her; she should know better."

Ah, in the name of culture or whatnot, Mrs. P. had difficulty being assertive about what she needed and wanted. In the end, she felt so resentful, more tired, and angry. We can't expect others to read our minds.

In the above example, I talked with Mrs. P. for a long time about this, and finally, we agreed that the right way to go about it would have been breaking the cultural bond and communicating assertively about what she wanted. And as an outcome, the guest likely might have said, "Oh my God, let me help," and they both would have had a good time, or the guest would have felt offended and left, but Mrs. P. still would have maintained her peace of mind, got her well-deserved rest and focused on her baby instead. Mrs. P. finally admitted that she didn't want the guest to see her as a rude and bad host, so Mrs. P. put herself in that position of entertaining her guest even if she wasn't able to. Mrs. P. pretended she was fine and smiled as she wasn't tired and her back wasn't hurting. Isn't this crazy?

Assertive communication is what we need. It's an excellent way to a happy and fulfilling life. We don't know why the guest didn't offer help when seeing the situation and acted so selfishly, but we are only responsible for ourselves, not how others behave. We can't expect others to do what we would like them to do without telling them our expectations. It's not healthy. Take responsibility for your happiness and your needs being met.

Building Trust /Opening Your Heart

Open your heart! It sounds like a dangerous thing to do. If you open your heart, you might get hurt. Most of us keep our hearts hidden deeply.

We try to protect ourselves from opening up to anyone with honesty because we have no control over what others might do. Our experience tells us that's not a good idea by reminding us of different people who have betrayed, have used, and disappointed us.

We have all been there; we have been hurt and betrayed, so it is very natural to want to protect ourselves from any future danger, and we do it the only way we know how. We close off our hearts, and we refuse to let anyone into our hearts. We get scared to be vulnerable if we show people who we are and how we feel. So we pretend under our smiles, and we keep people in the distance.

I know! I've been there; I opened my heart and have been hurt way too many times. Only a few people have shown their worth to me. It was difficult for me to let people in my life, including the one who's now my husband. I had a great wall protecting me, and it was difficult for people to get close to me past a certain point. Finally, I had to knock the great wall down, and what a relief it was. The wall was separating the people in my life and me.

I wanted to share this tool last because I wanted to present other tools to open your heart. You might ask, what wall are you talking about? I don't have any walls. The attitude that I talked about in the beginning is one type of wall. If you keep thinking: "it's not possible to find friends at this age," "it's not possible to make friends in this culture, they simply don't understand me—you are building a wall that prevents you from opening your heart to new people, out of fear that they might potentially hurt you.

Once you change your mind about your belief, set new boundaries, and know how to communicate your needs, it is easy to open your heart. It's easy to be with friends and family and to invite other new people into your life. However, to open your heart, you need to trust. How do you build trust? You can't just open your heart to anyone and hope they don't break it.

For a long time in my life, I was very naive; no matter how many times I got hurt or felt betrayed, I never knew how to protect myself from people that I never should have trusted. I believed if I trusted someone and let them know that I trusted them, things would be okay. So I trusted people first, then when they betrayed my trust, I shut them out of my life. It was a pattern for me because I didn't know any other way.

Until it dawned on me to let people in, set boundaries, and proceed with caution until they proved to be trustworthy. I learned this lesson only about seven years ago after feeling betrayed by a friend that I held close to my heart. She was like a sister to me.

Since then, I took control over how much I share and how much I trust people. It worked like magic. I never had to complain again.

While writing this part of the chapter, I was having coffee with Sara, a friend, and I told her what I was writing about. I then asked her what her thoughts were about trust and how she knows she can trust people.

She said, "Why trust people when you know they will betray you anyway?" I could sense the hurt she experienced by the pale color of her skin and the tone of her voice. She explained she found the right way: Not to trust anyone at all.

She continued, "I have been burned way too many times to trust anyone now. I am good. Thank you. I have my family and a few friends I trust. Other than that, I don't need to trust anyone else."

I can empathize with Sara; I've been there, done it many times. We all agree that we are social animals, so we need to make new connections to build a support system. However, shutting down entirely or trusting without reason will only lead to frustration, disconnection, and feeling alone.

People come in different colors, shapes, and behaviors, and you have no control over them. However, now that you have all the tools you need, you can open your heart and welcome new people into your life.

In the beginning, observe people intently and watch them repeatedly to see if they can be trustworthy. That is how you build trust; you don't trust people initially because they are pleasant or say you can trust them.

At first, share a little bit and see how they relate to what you tell them. See if the other person is sharing with you as much as you are communicating with him/her. If they are sharing less, then share less as well and give the friendship time to evolve. Some people don't like talking about themselves and their lives at the beginning of friendships. So respect that.

Next, start sharing a little more than you usually share and see how they react. Does the other person feel more connected to you and share with you as much as you share with him/her? If yes, the relationship is going more in-depth; if not, keep it where it is and nurture it. Some relationships take a long time to develop.

I have friends that I have an intense relationship with. We can talk about anything, any personal things that I wouldn't share with others. I have old friendships that are not that deep, but they are still friendships on some level, which also works. Observe and decide what kind of friendship it is. And meet people where they are.

And please let them know your boundaries when they cross them and observe if they respect your boundaries and respect your beliefs. Friendships take a long time to develop, and there are many layers to go deep in a relationship throughout the years. Don't rush it; let it take its sweet time to flourish. Understand as you become an expert at choosing people to be in your circle; choose only those you can trust, and keep building and maintaining the relationship. It will be worth your effort. You could be in a foreign country where you know no one from your original culture, and yet, you can open up to people because you know your boundaries and how to uphold them if crossed.

By now, you have learned how to say what you want and need, how to say no, and be open-minded. You could make friends who become family later, friends who have your back and might not even be from the culture where you grew up. True story! And you can enjoy your life comfortably, knowing that you have a support system that nourishes your life and that you are a part of a support system for others too. With all the tools you have, all you need is to trust yourself! Trust yourself only to let people who are worthy of your time and energy. And that, my friends, is the beginning of feeling at home in America.

Nurturing Your Relationships

Now that you know how to let emotionally healthy people in your life, you must learn how to maintain those connections. Relationships are like plants; they need watering and maintenance. If you have a big circle of friends and family as I do, it's essential to take extra time from your busy schedule to nurture these relationships. It could be by scheduling time to meet and talk if you live in the same city or regularly call each other to keep each other up to date.

Support your friends and family members in their hardships; it could be emotional support by sharing their experiences and listening to them. I meet friends who live close to me at least once a month for a movie, dinner, or lunch. We have fun, talk about what is going on in our lives and the kids. It is so much fun and mutually nurturing; besides, it's nice to get away from the mundane tasks of life to catch up. So we make sure to keep in touch and commit to our once-a-month date even with our busy schedules.

Some occasions get us together more. We give each other extra time to meet for sickness, the birth of a child, kids birthdays, and parents' birthdays to provide each other additional support. With those occasions, text time and calling increases till the situation subsides. Some of my friendships are far away, and our only communication method is the phone, Facetime, or Skype. However, we make sure we travel to see each other for special occasions, weddings, deaths, baptisms, etc.

This experience deepens the relationship and lets the other person know that they are not alone, that you are always there for their happiness and sadness as they are there for you. Although it took me a lot of time to figure out how to nurture and maintain friendships, now that I have been doing it for so long, it is the most fulfilling and rewarding part of friendship. Because in the process, both parties nurture each other.

If you have a friend you like, but you are giving more to them than them to you, you will likely end up feeling frustrated, resentful, and worn out. Friendship is a two-way street. Both parties need to carry the relationship.

When you find you're in a one-sided situation with your friends, meet them where they are, give only as much as they are offering, and if the situation changes, then adjust accordingly. In a good relationship, sometimes you would have to give more if the other person is going through some hardship. They would perhaps require more emotional support from you; that is part of friendship. You can't be a giver and a taker at the same time. As long as you know that once they figured out to live with the hardship, they would give back as much as you do. If you are in a situation where you need more support, you know you can count on them to give you more emotional support.

However, if some friends have shown you that they are only taking and not giving much support and only show up when they need something and are nowhere to be found when you need help, you need to cut them loose or downgrade the relationship. Otherwise, it will drain you. Be aware that some people can't give or be supportive. They know how to use people and are masters at getting your attention in other ways. They would make you feel guilty if you reduce the time you spend with them.

I avoid friends who try to make me feel guilty for not communicating with them. This type of friendship is not what I want in my life. We already have hectic lives with our jobs, kids, and life in general; even if you don't work, life in the US is hectic. It would help if you had friends who cheer you on and support you as you do for them and not friends that drain you and make your life miserable. If you have people like that in your life, just cut them off as you would a weed. Then find friends and relationships that nurture you and support you and reciprocate with goodness. You have no time to waste on friendships that don't work. These kinds of friendships will distract you from your goals and make your cultural integration process difficult.

CHAPTER 7

SKILLSET #5: ATTITUDE ABOUT MONEY

What is money?

When I was getting ready to write this chapter, I started browsing the internet to see what people think about money. I was amazed to see so many famous people describing their opinion about money. I found many quotes about money. It dawned on me that none of them gave us a definition of money but shared their relationship with it. We all have a different relationship with money, whether we like it or not. We have learned it from our parents or our culture, or we picked up our own along our way.

Whether we learned it this way or that way, our belief about money, which is usually unconscious, determines how we spend or keep the money. If this wasn't true, then we should all agree with the definition of money and shouldn't see it as anything other than its meaning, which is:

Something generally accepted as a medium of exchange, a measure of value, or a means of payment: such as coin, paper money. (Merriam-Webster Dictionary)

It seems to me that money is just a form of exchange. I like the dress I see in the store, and I want to buy it, I purchase the dress with cash or use my credit card, and take my dress home. But those paper notes and coins seem actually to occupy our minds greatly. Sometimes all day. The thoughts in our minds about money are not the same for everybody. If you think for a moment, we all have a particular idea and belief in our mind about money, and it is personal.

When I was writing this book, I asked five random people to tell me what they had been thinking and believing about money for the last week. Below are the responses I received:

- I don't have enough money
- We should save more money this month
- I worry I don't have enough money for retirement
- How can I earn more money so that I can retire comfortably?
- My husband and I were talking about finances last night, and our conversation about it was, "Where should we cut down so we can save more money?"

Writing this was fascinating because it helped me see my money mentality and belief compared to five years ago. Yes, our money beliefs can change, and it is an ever-changing and evolving process.

How we spend and save depends on our belief system. I know! I thought this was crazy, too!

Unhealthy/Healthy Beliefs About Money

The first one that comes to my mind is: "Money is the cause of all evils." I am from a Christian background, so I know that my unhealthy belief about money came from my religious experience. It took me years to realize that the teaching "money is evil" had become part of my belief system, which I had to break free from. We will explore more later, but for now, let's identify other unhealthy beliefs.

Other unhealthy beliefs that are common are:

- You have to work hard and save hard
- Rich people are not good people
- Money is there to spend
- Money is not important; it is selfish to want more money
- It's a sin to pray for money
- Be either rich or happy, but you can't be both
- The poor will go to heaven, but it will be hard for rich people to do so

If we dig deep enough, you will find so many unhealthy beliefs we hold about money, and unfortunately, those beliefs run our lives and rob us of having the fulfilling lives we want. I know it's a bizarre idea if you had never heard of it before, I felt the same way when I heard it for the first time. It's a normal reaction.

Six years ago, I had a belief that no matter how much money I earned or saved, it wasn't enough. I always needed more. I needed to take my son for stem cell therapy and I wanted to take him to an expensive, private physical therapist. Plus, there were the everyday bills and, at the end of the day, I had nothing I could save for the future. Thinking about my retirement was out of the question. I was struggling with the basic survival needs. Money issues caused me more stress than any happiness.

While under all the stress, I read that our belief about money dictates the quality of life we lead. At first, I thought it was a bunch of baloney (nonsense) because that would mean I am responsible for where I am in life today by choice. Why would anyone choose to be stressed about money? Why would they settle on just surviving? Because if it were up to me, I would want to choose less stress and more money. Then, again, that is the thing about radical ideas; even if you don't believe them at first, they don't leave you. The more I thought about it, the more curious I got. I started seeing it everywhere. I went to a self-development class and heard about that idea again, I would be reading a book, and there it was too.

Finally, I confronted myself and started exploring what my belief about money was. Then I was like a computer search engine: thoughts started flying in my head, quotes I heard from someone, from my family, my friends, something I read in a book. I was so surprised to look at this reality.

Growing up with my father being an engineer and my cousin who grew up with me, who is like my brother, and being married to an engineer, I realized I had a very rational mind. If I can't see it, I don't believe it, which was why, when I was younger, I had to search in every religion to find God.

I saw that experience about my belief, with me summoning it, made me realize we are like computers with programming that is downloaded from our family, friends, culture, and other things. My rational mind was amazed at what it discovered.

Here are some of the beliefs I found I had which I never realized before:

- Money doesn't grow on trees
- You must work hard and save hard
- Money comes with sweat and blood
- You can't serve money
- God is good and money is evil
- Give all you have to the poor
- There is not enough money
- Asking for money will get you in trouble,
- Money can cause divorce
- Money can cause friction
- Money isn't good
- Don't think about money otherwise you will not go to heaven

I also remember different images of my parents dealing with money and other people I've known, so my mind drew some of the conclusions from seeing that, and it had become a belief.

It's no wonder I was struggling, it was like I needed money, but I was afraid of having more. It was like I wanted money, but I hated money. What you hate and don't respect won't come to your home. I mean, if you keep treating someone you know with disrespect and show them you don't like them, they wouldn't visit you, would they? Same with money.

I was surprised to discover all these beliefs about money that I never knew I had. I read that beliefs we hold about anything are stored in our subconscious. I don't think I understood my Psychology 101 in my second year at university when we studied the subconscious mind.

I realized what people are talking about when they say, "We create our reality." I still have many issues to work out with that sentence, but at least when it comes to money, addiction, and relationships, I have found this to be true.

After that, it was easy to confront my beliefs, examine them, and from where I stand now, knowing what I know today, ask myself: Is this belief true for me? Surprisingly, most of those beliefs weren't real for me. The minute I recognized them, like magic, the beliefs went away. Next, I started telling myself what I wanted to believe about money. It was like throwing old furniture out of my house and replacing it with new things.

Here are some of my current money beliefs:

- Yes, money grows on a tree (through ideas)
- Yes, money feels good
- Money pays for the beautiful home I live in

- Money pays for the car that I drive to work, to meet my friends, or do something important in my life
- Money paid for this computer I am writing to share my ideas and experiences that will make a difference
- Money paid for my plane ticket to come to this country that is giving me all the wonderful opportunities to live my life by design
- Money bought the beautiful sweater my son is wearing that is making him so handsome right now that it is making me want to play with him
- Money let us buy a ticket and visit our family in Italy. I had a great time with them, ate Italian food, and learned from their culture
- Money lets me buy any program I want to learn about a topic
- Money lets my family hire someone to babysit my boy, who is playing in the next room happily while I am writing this book so I can make a profound impact on people's lives and pursue my passion for sharing what I've learned and know so far
- Money lets me put gas in my car
- Money lets my family buy all the fresh food, including all the yummy vegetables that I bought to make lunch in about an hour
- Money is not bad
- Money is a tool to help me
- Money is our family's friend, a good friend that I can go to and say, hey, I want to buy this today, and it says sure, here you go!
- I love what money can do! I love money! That's right! I love money. I don't keep what I don't love in my life.

Don't get me wrong, I don't worship money, but I respect it for its role and the excellent tool it is in my life. As soon as I realized new beliefs on money, I defined my relationship with it. Everything changed. Believe it or not, after four years, my life changed dramatically; my income doubled and tripled.

If you are like me, I am a rational person; reading this, you may think, what is she talking about? How can realizing something change anything?

Changing your belief and relationship with money is just the first part of the process. Remember I said after six years, things changed in my life? That is because it involves work, yes, hard work! I am sure you have been doing it all your life. However, this time, the reward is sweeter because you come from a different belief that serves you. Now, you are not sweating to survive but to improve your finances and keep going to feel abundant and prosperous in your life. The American dream!

Realizing this fact was huge for me, after that day, I woke up every morning with excitement and not dreading my day, knowing that my dreams are possible.

I enrolled in self-development classes, got a mentor, invested, and received clarity on the steps I needed to take to stay focused on my plan. Some of the exams were so tough; it took three times to pass and succeed. I put in the hard work to turn my life in a new direction, and now I look at and marvel at the progress. It's like seeing a gardener looking at the blooming flowers he worked so hard to cultivate last spring.

I am not saying I'm where I want to be, not yet, but I am now where I need to be. I want to accomplish so many things in my lifetime, but I am not afraid to take the baby steps to get there while looking at the fruits and flowers of my labor. And I feel confident I will get where I am going next. I am on a journey!

You must know where you are going is achievable by using your talents and hard work as long as your money beliefs are in alignment with supporting your life.

My Worrier Friend and Squandering Colleague

Here are more examples of how our money belief is related to the lives we currently lead.

Gail was a college friend, an immigrant from Peru, who had always worried about money for the ten years I had known her. None of her fears came true, but Gail kept running with that fear. Going to a restaurant eating with her was not a fun experience because she wanted to order the cheapest item on the menu, and wanted us to do the same. Gail stressed so much that she stressed me out with her conversation about lack of money.

One day she shared with me that her mom always complained about money and how they didn't have enough. Without realizing it, Gail had become like her mom. I asked if her belief about money came from her mother? She automatically connected the dots; it was an "aha moment" and the most life-changing conversation she ever had. Gail said it was not because of anything I did, but the question made her realize her way of being had become exactly like her mom.

Currently, Gail is doing what she loves, and her dream is to be a millionaire, ha! That's quite a shift of perspective, and I haven't heard her complain about money again. And I do believe she can achieve her goals. I want to be her friend, so maybe I will be treated to upscale restaurants! Jokingly, I deserve it for putting up with all the complaining. But seriously, all jokes aside, our life is run by a belief system you may no longer believe in now. Some of the belief systems resulted from something that happened a long time ago when you were a kid or a teenager. You may want to revisit your belief systems regularly so you can always have a healthy relationship with money that will, in return, give you a different result in your life.

Here is another story about my squandering colleague, Lila, from Nigeria. I have her permission to share this story. We changed her name for privacy reasons. Lila is a sweet person who is so good at heart. I love her caring nature, and we have been very close colleagues for many years. Throughout the years, she had no problem earning money, but nothing seemed to stick. She never had the money for anything. She had been homeless quite a few times because she couldn't keep up with her rent money by the end of the month.

I lent Lila money, which she promised to pay back but never did. It put a lot of strain on our relationship in the past. It took me a couple of years to say no to her because as much as Lila meant that she would pay it back, she never did. So, I had to put my foot down and gave up the thought of wanting her to pay back what she owed me. I was a big believer, and I still am, that "What goes around comes around," what you give out comes back to you. It is one belief I don't want to change. So, at some point, I saw my friend Lila less and less because hanging out with her meant paying for everything everywhere we went after work or at lunchtime.

After I learned about my belief system, I had a talk with Lila about my experience one day. She thought it was weird, but she was intrigued enough to continue the conversation. Lila wanted to find out what her beliefs were about money.

We did an exercise where she was to start the sentence with "My money belief is . . ." She broke down in tears. Lila said money is nothing; money is evil; you shouldn't give money any importance, whether prosperous or happy. She told me she could even hear her dad's voice saying it.

It was a wake-up call for her. Lila is a hard-working person and brilliant. However, she thought of choosing happiness over money and didn't know she could do both on a subconscious level. However, on the conscious level, Lila was struggling and was wondering what was wrong with her. Other people her age seemed to have the things she wanted and didn't seem to struggle as she did.

With that realization, Lila is now unrecognizable. She changed her belief about money not being important and hired a financial adviser to manage her money and assets. Lila took classes on money management, learned a healthy way of spending and saving. She was finally in control of her finances and got rid of the unhealthy belief that was robbing her of the life she wanted to have. I remember my surprise when Lila called me a few years ago and said, "Hey, I want to meet for lunch." She paid for both our lunches and gave me the money I lent her many years ago with a "thank you for putting up with me" card. I found out that she had done that with all the people that had helped her out over the years, letting everybody know, "Hey, I know I screwed up, but I got this now. I can handle my life now and here is the proof."

It blew my mind. Lila changed her beliefs about money, started a new relationship with it, and when she did, her life automatically changed. Yes, it took hard work, a few years of investing in herself, learning new things, writing her resume to get another higher paying job, and going on interviews. Lila probably had to spend extra time than the average person to catch up on her life. Still, the result was worth the effort. Can you imagine that Lila didn't lose any of her friends? If that wasn't a miracle, I don't know what is.

It is why I love doing what I do; I want to inspire and empower immigrants like myself. Everything we dream about, everything that pushes us to come to our new country is possible with a few adjustments in our belief system and hard work. It delights me to share my journey, experience, and what I learned during my cultural integration process.

Transforming Your Attitude About Money

It's your turn to transform your belief about money, just like Gail, Lila, and I, plus many other people I know. Are you ready? If you are, here is your first tool.

Tool #1

Find a quiet place, get your pen and paper, sit and write the following:

My money belief is _____

_____

_____

_____

Write whatever comes to your mind. Get it out: the right beliefs, wrong beliefs. Keep at it. Suppose you get stuck like I sometimes do when I have paper in front of me to write something, my mind freezes. Just write anything that comes to your mind. If it's something silly, write it down. If you feel like, "I don't know if this is going to work," write it down. Once you get good at writing whatever comes to your mind, then go back to the statement, and write your beliefs.

Money is _____

_____

_____

_____

After you have written all your beliefs about Money, examine all of them, one by one. Acknowledge this is how you have been functioning all your life when it comes to your finances.

If you feel unintelligent, and your mind is trying to put you down and make you feel embarrassed about your past choices.

Have compassion for yourself, like you would have understanding for a baby who just started to walk and is stumbling and frustrated. Tell yourself you have done everything you could to make it work with the knowledge you had in the past.

I remember having so many tears when I did this exercise, so if you feel like crying, cry and let it out. If you feel upset, punch a pillow and let it out. If you feel silly, hold yourself and give yourself a lot of love and comfort as you would give to your best friend. What you just did is something to be proud of. Be very proud that you were willing to change.

Tool #2

After you finish, either the same day or the next, take as much time as you need. Examine the beliefs; take what will serve you, and let go of what doesn't. Nothing is required for the things you no longer need; acknowledge your new belief and celebrate; the old belief is gone. If it creeps up again in your thoughts, you will recognize it, smile, and say, "I don't believe this anymore," and repeat to yourself your new beliefs. If you don't have enough positive thoughts about money, adopt other ideas, which we did as kids. We adopted different views as our own unconsciously, but now, you are doing it with a choice that can benefit you for sure this time.

Here are more positive money beliefs:

- There is enough money in the world for everyone
- Rich people get rich because they are wise investors and see opportunities where others see obstacles
- Feeling financially secure, I'm in a better position to give to others.
- Money is my friend. Money is good. Money allows me to enjoy the lifestyle my family and I have.

You can use mine or determine the beliefs about the money of the wealthiest people you admire and adopt those beliefs as your own. As I previously mentioned, when I did the exercise, I felt resistance, and thoughts from my religious background came back, telling me what Jesus said. Although I did the exercise, I didn't believe it 100%. I felt guilty every time I did it. I felt like I was betraying my Christian background, and then I stumbled on this quote by the Dalai Lama:

"Money is good. It is important. Without money, daily survival—not to mention further development—is impossible. So we are not even questioning its importance. At the same time, it is wrong to consider money a god or a substance endowed with some power of its own. To think that money is everything and that having lots of it will solve our problems is a serious mistake."

The Dalai Lama's words resonated with me, so I researched the Bible scriptures to find positive things written about money. I finally understood that God wasn't talking about money being evil. That erroneous belief didn't make sense because many people in the Bible, except Jesus and His disciples (their purpose was different), were blessed by abundance and riches.

Other than that, I found out that those who obey God, work hard, don't worship money, and don't love money for more than what it can give and provide them, are blessed. If you are Christian and your belief is holding you back, here is one scripture I found while writing this book:

> *The Lord will open the heavens, the storehouse of his bounty, to send rain on your land in season and to bless all the work of your hands. You will lend to many nations but will borrow from no one.*
>
> *Deuteronomy 28:12*

The Bible is full of scriptures that tell how God will reward those who are honest and obey His laws, are not greedy, and enjoy giving. It also says that He disciplines the greedy, and that it's easier for a camel to go through the eye of a needle than for a rich man to enter the kingdom of God. Here, of course, He is referring to greed and not money or riches.

Also, I have heard from my Muslim friends that Islam scripture (The **Qur'an**) is full of warnings against greed and dishonest dealings in business, and of blessings for those that are honest and don't dwell on deceiving others in the hope of getting money.

I found this from Islam's questions and answers on the internet:

Narrated from Abu Sa'eed al-Khudri (may Allah be pleased with him) that the Messenger of Allah (peace and blessings of Allah be upon him) said: "The honest, trustworthy merchant will be with the Prophets, siddeeqs, and martyrs."

You can read more about it here:

https://islamqa.info/en/answers/77225/the-hadeeth-every-merchant -will-enter-hell-except-those-who-are-pious

So whatever religious beliefs and thoughts you follow, I invite you to go back to the writings of your Holy books; and examine, question, and educate yourself about the wrong beliefs you have been holding to discard the ones that are holding you back. The truth is we were misinformed; it doesn't matter what the reason behind it is.

Several books provide trustworthy advice on managing our money, avoiding debt, and not falling into being greedy and boastful because of what we have. I enjoy reading Holy books written long ago and have wisdom and insight into our world today. That is why you need to examine everything until it gets clear in your mind and there is no conflict within yourself.

Now that we have that out of the way. Let's proceed to the next step, which is how to change your current situation. Please know that just because you change your belief, it doesn't mean the food will appear on the table from nothing with a snap of your fingers or waving a wand, and there is nothing you need to do. Maybe that is what happens in Harry Potter books and movies, but we don't live in a fictional world. You have a lot of work ahead of you. And that is ok.

Tool #3

Write down on a piece of paper what you want and what is preventing you from achieving it.

I want a lot of money but _____

_____

_____

_____

I want a bigger apartment but _____

_____

_____

_____

I want _____

_____

_____

_____

But _____

_____

_____

_____

Although you might discover some more unhealthy money beliefs here, you mostly will find what is in the way of you getting what you want, and now with your harmful beliefs out of the way, you can finally see actions you need to take.

For instance, you may discover that you want a bigger apartment, but you can't afford it. Ask a follow-up question. "Why can't I afford it?" the answer may be, "I can't afford it because my job doesn't pay me enough." There lies the problem. My job doesn't pay me enough is where the problem is and what is in your way. Now that you have identified the problem, the next step might be to get a raise where you work right now, assuming you are happy there, or get another job that will pay you more.

Your next steps may be, for example:

- Thinking and rehearsing how you can ask your boss for a raise
- It could be researching how to get another job while you are still working
- Attend a job fair and search for employment with another company to satisfy your financial needs
- Enroll in training on how to update and improve your resume

Now that you have identified your issue, get an action plan to take care of that problem for you to move to a bigger apartment. It may take longer than what you plan; however, be patient with yourself, and you will get there. I promise.

When you're headed in the right direction with clarity, commitment, patience, and consistency, you will see things shifting and different new opportunities presenting themselves to help you further with your commitment. I know this might not feel like a rational thing to say and it may not seem to make logical sense, but I have experienced it in my life and with many others. I marvel at the way things work out all the time. I believe everything can be explained, even if we haven't found a way to describe it yet. However, until I do, I will say miracles will happen to move you from where you are to where you want to be as long as you are clear about the problem and the actions you need to take to move from point A to B. When you take consistent steps towards the goal, it has no option but to happen.

When I was introduced to this exercise, I was already working hard in making sure I was making ends meet and I could pay my rent, take care of my disabled child, and put food on the table without help from anyone or any government body.

At that time, I found out that although Aaron was disabled, because he wasn't a US citizen yet, he didn't qualify for Social Security; things were tough on me being a single mom with a special needs child, paying rent by myself, and working two jobs. The problem I had was that although I worked two jobs, I wasn't paid enough to have a saving.

After doing the above exercise, I determined that the solution to my problem was I needed to be a certified court interpreter. I discovered that, by being certified, I could almost double the money I was earning at one job, enabling me to quit the other position. The decision would allow me to focus on Aaron's ever-demanding life and give me breathing space to myself and to do other things I love.

Then I asked the question: What can I do? Answer: Get a certification for one of the jobs I was already doing to almost double my salary. Action: I bought the books I needed and studied. Result: I got certified, have only one job, quit the other job, and have more time to spend with my son and myself.

So follow the steps:

1. Recognize your issue
2. Identify what to do
3. Prepare for the change—take action
4. Enjoy the result

Of course, this didn't happen in one day. I had to make the time to study to take the national exam to be a registered court interpreter in the State of California. I failed on my first try because I was not putting enough time in to study. Not because I didn't want to, but because I didn't have enough time.

I worked two jobs when Aaron went to school and daycare (two hours after school). After I came home, I had to do all that my son needed: feed him, bathe him, change him, do his home physical therapy, then spend some quality time with him before I put him to bed at 9 p.m. My mom was a tremendous help to me in caring for Aaron during that time. Often, I could skip some of the things that I had to do for him, which gave me an hour or so to spare for studying, depending on the day.

When Aaron went to sleep, I would then spend time returning emails, scheduling appointments for him or rescheduling them if needed, and managing quite a busy schedule. I would then spend half an hour studying before going to sleep. I would wake up the same morning to repeat the same thing. Then something miraculous happened: I got my citizenship (for which I had applied a year earlier), making Aaron a citizen automatically. Within just a few months, he received benefits that he previously didn't qualify for. That gave me some breathing space financially.

I left my other job and enrolled in a year-long program to develop some of the skills I needed to learn, such as focus, multitasking, productivity, and time management. I bought a book and a CD to help me study effectively in my area. Then I set aside two hours to study every day, five days a week. "Boom," I passed the exam. I tell you it was a sweet victory.

My income doubled, allowing me to free myself from most government aid for Aaron, including Social Security supplemental income. I was self-sufficient, living a dream life with my son without needing anyone's help. I remember feeling so proud and happy about my achievements.

While my life was transforming, I met the love of my life, and we decided to get married, which made my living situation even more comfortable for our growing family.

Notice the sequence of events that happened to help me get where I wanted to be when I decided to take action in the face of failure and the lack of time. As long as we embrace our commitment and keep going, things have a mysterious way of helping us achieve our goals and many other sweet surprises along the way. The more we persist, the more results occur that carry us through to achieve what we intended to do.

Government Aid

One thing I love about this country is that when you have tried your best and can't handle life for whatever reason, there are so many resources to help you.

I like to think of things in images, and when I think of resources, including government aid, I imagine myself as an injured football player. Emergency medical technicians (EMTs) rush on the field with their gurney and first aid kit to help. The techs move me on the gurney to the sidelines to take care of me and determine if my injury is severe enough to take to me the hospital. Or they recommend any aid to assist with my healing.

I would assume I'm helped while I recover.

I grew up watching the World Cup soccer game every four years with my dad. I have kept this tradition to this day. I am fascinated by how the players withstand and persevere to play and win. I happen to love stories of triumph after injuries or life-threatening issues. I have many stories that have inspired me, but I will share two of them with you.

Petr Cech, a soccer goalkeeper, was not only at risk of losing his career from an accident during a game in 2006; his life was actually in danger from a severe skull fracture. However, he returned to the top. He went back on the field just three months after the accident and re-established himself as one of the best goalkeepers in the world, breaking the Premier League's all-time clean sheet record in 2015.

Another football player that inspires me is Nwankwo Kanu: this Nigerian soccer player was born with a severe heart defect, which he overcame. In 1996 he underwent open-heart surgery to replace an aortic valve, and he returned to play only six months later. After that, he played with significant European soccer teams such as Inter and Arsenal. In 1999 he was named African Footballer of the Year.

I can go on and on; I bet these men were discouraged and did not imagine they could do what they did before being hit with misfortune. Perhaps people in their lives, seeing the severity of their condition, tried to convince them to stop trying and be comfortable with their situation, and maybe they said this with love.

But these men didn't fall for the trap of comfort. They took the time they needed to recover and went back to their games.

I love reading inspiring stories of people like that.

If you play soccer for a living, you are sure to run into injuries of all kinds, but you can never quit and leave the game for good. By the same token, if you take life like a soccer game, I know it's tempting to feel discouraged, but I urge you to never give up on yourself, no matter how much misfortune life throws at you.

When I continued studying even harder after I quit my other job and got some financial help for my son, I was asked by five different people why I was still learning. Someone even tried to give me advice saying, "Now that you have the aid, why don't you rest when you don't have Aaron and he is at school. I know your life is tough, so why struggle more? You need to be careful once you start earning more money; you may lose the benefits for your son and yourself. Why are you going to the library to study hard as if you don't have enough on your plate?"

I understood my adviser wasn't trying to hurt or discourage me. He was trying to help me ease my situation, understanding my situation with my son, and telling me that what I was doing was already enough. He was trying to assure me no one would blame me for not doing more or succeeding more. He felt that as long as my basic needs and bills are covered, I could live a comfortable life. I thanked him and felt the love he was trying to show, but I saw the trap of comfort for what it was. I told him politely that I appreciate his concern and care and that I love and value his kindness.

Although I saw his perspective and knew it was an option, I said, "I didn't come to America to be comfortable. I have big dreams within me that don't let me sleep at night, and I believe with time and dedication I will be able to achieve them all, even if it takes me 20 years more."

I will never forget the look on his face. Shock, fascination, embarrassment, but most of all, I saw a light bulb light up in his eyes. Although this man lived in this country for 20+ years when we had that conversation, from his look, I could tell he never heard that before or he never thought like that before. I don't know what happened to this person after that conversation, but I hope that was a life-changing conversation for him as it was for me.

Don't fall into the trap of comfort, and don't play it safe, even if that's what everyone you know is doing in your community. Of course, it was scary to lose my son's social security income and other benefits because of my income increase. However, things worked out as they were supposed to. And I knew that even if circumstances changed, the aid was available in its place. I didn't have to stay stuck in it, limiting what I could be in life.

The same conversation happened when I decided to get married after I found the love of my life. We were both hurt in the past and were frustrated in finding the right person. It was such a delight when we finally found each other, and we both wanted the same thing—get married, build a family, and live our lives together. Everything was unfolding smoothly, and we were following our hearts.

Of course, we had to do our diligent work to see how our decision might impact each other's life since I already had a child with a disability. We talked about it, and I understood I had to give up certain benefits that I still had left.

I understood I had to let go of many beneficial things in my life that helped me up until that point to pursue the happiness I wanted. You see, you can't have it both ways. You can't make your life great and at the same time hide behind benefits and aids. The aids and services are there until the opportunities to be more than you are at the moment present themselves. Besides, we should take pride in working hard to get ourselves off of government aid. Because, culturally, in the US, that is celebrated! As it should be. When you get off social assistance, it's because you are becoming more than what you were, and everybody recognizes it took hard work and a lot of effort on your part.

So after doing our research for a year, we got married in City Hall with just one friend present. Later we sent out invitations to our family, friends, and people we wanted at our wedding ceremony to celebrate our happiness after eight months of our marriage.

Then we were flooded with comments. One I remember is a woman who has four kids and one on the way, said to me, "Why are you getting married? You can still get married but not legally so you can keep your benefits for yourself and your kids." I felt deeply sorry for this person. She lived her life small, not knowing her potential, afraid to pursue the things she wanted legally; she might not make it in life. The worst part of it was she didn't know this. She thought she knew everything about getting ahead in life and gave me genuine advice out of love and concern for me. Except she was asking me to remain small and play it safe.

I didn't know what to say, and I didn't want to hurt her feelings. So I started walking away without saying anything. Instantly I needed to say something to her to make her think and maybe transform her life. So, I told her, "I didn't come to America to remain at the mercy of governmental aid. I came for abundance and to prosper. The road of government benefits helped me to get there, and I'm thankful, but it isn't the road of abundance and prosperity for my family and me."

She was defensive and replied: "Well, I was just trying to help you." She left. I knew she was indeed trying to help me, and she meant nothing wrong by it. And I am sure she was coming from a place of love. But I needed to speak my truth, and I hope it will help her think about our conversation as it did for me. It changed me and made me curious enough to teach this to others who may encounter people like her when they come to their new country.

I get it; it's so scary to let go of benefits once you have them. I've been there. Like I previously said, I was afraid to let go of what is, for what it could be, and I can tell you I have never been happier. I live in a place of happiness. It doesn't mean there are no challenges, but now I have a second mind to solve them. My kids are much happier, and we work as hard as ever to keep moving to our milestone of abundance and prosperity together. It's a journey and not a destination!

Most of all, I don't have to fake anything. I hate the effort that hiding something takes; it would cause me a lot of stress. It would take a lot of energy to hide something either from someone or a government. Living life takes a lot of energy as it is; why would I want to spend unnecessary energy worrying that maybe they will find out or track my steps to lead them to what I am hiding? My God that would be like living in prison. I love to live my life in freedom.

In my life, I adopted one of my neighbor's sayings growing up in Africa. "It's better to be honest and be homeless than lie and sleep in a luxurious house."

The more I live in that wisdom, the more I understand what it means. It means as long as you speak the truth, even if you are homeless, you will sleep soundly and in peace and not care. But if you tell a lie or withhold information you are trying to cover up, your sleep will not be peaceful even if you sleep in a big house. As a follower of this wisdom from my childhood neighbor, I can tell you, once you free up your energy from withholding, covering up, and be honest not only with the government but with people, your life will be much simpler. Because now you can use all that energy you would have to spend on covering up and worrying, for something better, something useful, like building your life and making it as you want it to be.

I can recall a case at a criminal court about a guy; we will call him John. He had been in the US for only four years. John was married with three kids and charged with fraud. The court asked him to pay a lot of money, which he had already started paying slowly. John was worried about the seriousness of the fraud charge against him. When I met him, he trembled, rubbing his hands together and sweating profusely, although it was early in the morning.

John said to me while we were waiting for his attorney, "I will never listen to what people advise me from now on." He told me that when his wife had the baby, they applied for governmental benefits, which they received. After his wife started working, he was told by some people that they could continue to collect the financial aid until the child was five-years-old. He said that he felt uneasy with that but didn't check if this was solid advice. He trusted what his friends told him and continued to take the government's money, although both his wife and he had full-time salaries.

After a few months, when he had an appointment with their caseworker, he notified her that his wife had started working. Sure enough, he was asked to return the money they received for the past eight months because they no longer qualified. Although it was a lot of money, the guy didn't mind paying off slowly, but he was shocked to discover, on top of that, he was charged with fraud.

I am sure John signed a form explaining his rights and responsibilities when he applied for the benefits. However, we don't always read all the paperwork presented to us as new immigrants because it's overwhelming. We don't ask for an interpreter because we feel proud and don't think we need assistance.

John honestly didn't know. What's worse is, the people who advised him, who had lived here for a long time, most probably didn't know either. Yes, we have to be aware of what advice we get from people. However, don't just trust them because they lived in the US longer than you have. It doesn't make them an expert in anything. Always double-check. My husband often brings up President Ronald Reagan's quote: "Trust but verify." I believe this saying applies here. Always double-check what you hear from your community with your social worker or the authority figure that handles your case.

Luckily for John, his attorney understood what was going on and fought for him, so he didn't have any criminal charge against him, which could have ruined his life. He won. He got lucky! Lucky because his attorney was competent and believed it was an unfortunate situation.

Please stay away from people who tell you to depend on government aid when you are capable of working and living a full life. Use government aid only when you need it. You can make money in the US working full time, part-time, being an entrepreneur, and you can definitely make your life work.

Managing Your Money

Managing your money is another area that our education system didn't teach us growing up. So we rely on our skills that came from our parents or our immediate surroundings.

After you move to the US or even before, you might examine your money management skills if you haven't already. You may find out that you have some excellent money skills and other areas you need to improve. That's perfect because if you have reached a place where you feel you know your strength and your weakness when it comes to money management, then you know exactly what area you need to invest your time to learn new skills to get your finances in order.

As I said before, there is nothing to be ashamed of in admitting what you don't know. You have moved to the US, which means your life has gotten more complicated than you can imagine. You will see things you don't even know how to pronounce, let alone know how to do. It is just part of the process and if you are in that place, know that all immigrants to this new country had to go through precisely what you are going through. There is no shame in it.

My Money Management Tips

1. Build your credit scores

In America, you need to build your credit score to achieve anything. Here is a story my husband Marco and I like to tell when we talk about culture shock.

After arriving from Italy, Marco took a job in Silicon Valley. He needed to rent an apartment. With his busy work schedule, Marco would go to different apartments to look at ones he liked. Soon Marco was shocked to discover that the landlords/property managers asked if he had a good credit score. Marco told them he was new in the USA, and in Italy, there is no such thing as credit scores, so obviously, he didn't have it.

He was bummed with this unreasonable request. After so many frustrations, he finally met a landlord who was an immigrant from Taiwan. The man understood what my husband was telling him because he had the same problem when he first came to the US a long time ago. He was willing to rent Marco his condo.

As a new immigrant, not having a credit score is tough: without any way to prove to banks, and even landlords, that you are trustworthy, you may struggle to get an apartment lease, mortgage, or car loan.

You have to make sure to keep all your credit cards active and payments up-to-date. With no credit history you would have to sign up for a "secured credit card," essentially a limited credit card guaranteed by a refundable deposit. Provided that you keep re-paying your debt consistently every month, then the more you use the credit card, the more your credit score will increase. All other premiums or bills need to be kept up-to-date to build your credit score. Purchasing a car through monthly payments is also a good option to build credit. At some point you would be able to request an unsecured credit card.

However, don't fall into the belief that having a credit card means you have more money available to spend. You don't want to fall into debt, which would prevent you from achieving your American dream.

I know, I know, one of your culture shocks may be how Americans like to shop, shop and shop. We all have to fight the temptations that are purposely designed by hard marketing to hook us into the habit of buying. However, resist this urge as much as you can. Suppose you keep overspending, and you can't resist the temptation to buy impulsively. In that case, I suggest you give your credit card to your spouse or a good-trusted friend to hold until you develop a "muscle" to resist your over-spending urges and keep working on yourself.

2. Write Your Priorities

What is your first priority? Write down the most important items that you need to take care of now. Such as your rent, food, transportation, etc., and put that money aside. If you struggle with putting money aside, a skill set we all need to learn, set up automatic payments for all your essential bills, which means money is deducted automatically from your bank account or credit cards on a specific date.

One of my clients, who we will call Paula, struggled with overspending. Paula couldn't figure out why the money she made wasn't enough by the end of the month to pay for her essential bills. She told me after paying rent; it was hard to put food on the table. Paula was tired of struggling and told me how she didn't like this country, that it's all about paying bills and nothing more. We sat down and took care of her priorities first. We set up all of her important accounts on auto payments. It worked like a charm.

It doesn't mean we don't want to spend on other things than paying bills. Understandably, we would like to invest in something fancy; we might want to visit our hometown because we miss everyone we left behind. Sometimes those urges might be hard to resist, but they might compromise our goal to achieve our dreams. When those urges are strong, sit down with a piece of paper and write down those things you want to do: it might be traveling, buying a brand new car, etc. Then put those on a "save for later" list. Once you can pay all your bills, you have your life together and get it where you feel comfortable, which might take anywhere from five to ten years, then you will be ready to start checking off your save-for-later list.

3. Unburden Yourself

Most immigrants carry the burden of financially supporting their family they left behind. This burden almost crippled me financially when I first moved to the US. I was sending money every month, and I was struggling to have my basic needs met.

210

It's understandable to look back and see the situation you left behind. And you may feel guilty whenever you have money, and you need to spend it on yourself. Therefore you might have decided to send money to your family and other people that struggle back home to ease their situation.

I have met and seen many immigrants feeling so depressed because they can't get out of assisting their family back home while making their life in the US work because of their commitment out of guilt.

I also have coached clients who struggle because their family back home puts pressure on them with unreasonable expectations of receiving money. They would guilt them or withhold their love and emotional support when they don't receive money. The US relatives feel stuck because they can't meet both obligations: to support their family back home and make their life work here in America. So they feel resentful and angry and see no light at the end of the tunnel.

Reading this, I know you might nod your head and feel burdened by this responsibility. I will tell you exactly what I say to my clients; you may not like me coaching you on this, and that is ok. It isn't an easy lesson to learn; however, it's one that is inevitable. You will know it, whether it takes you five or twenty years. I would like you to be open-minded. Learn and apply this early on so you can avoid a lot of heartache in the process.

So, here are my tips to get yourself unstuck from this sticky situation:

I am sure you have heard the saying, "put on your mask first before you help someone else." You have probably heard it 100 times. When you fly on an airplane, the flight attendant instructs you to put on your oxygen mask first before helping others.

That saying also applies to your finances, meaning, have your life in order, be in a position to give to yourself first before giving; otherwise, you're not going to help yourself nor your family back in your home country in a sustainable way.

First, get your life in order. Don't try to explain to your family back home why you can't assist them since they will not understand you. One client said to me when coaching him: "but my family thinks money grows on trees in America, and whatever I say, they think I am lying."

It's true, only you know the US's situation, and don't blame them for not understanding that fact since they can't comprehend the life you lead here in America.

If important people in your hometown withhold their love, and you feel emotionally unsupported, use the tips I gave you earlier on expanding your support system. It will help you get the emotional support you need from people who understand you and your circumstances.

If you feel guilty about not giving back, make a list of people you would like to help once you are in a position to do so.

The other tip I want to give you is: learn what true giving means. Just sending money to your family or relatives to ease your guilt or to avoid their withholding of love isn't true giving. I was also guilty of doing that in the past.

True giving is when you make a difference to someone or a cause that would make a sustainable change in that person or people you are trying to help. Once you get your life in order, and you have more time and more money, you will be able to give in a meaningful way. For example, giving might also consist of solving a problem in your hometown. I know of a person from Tanzania who has a nonprofit organization that helps kids in the village she left behind to go to school by providing money for their school supplies, transportation, and clothes. When my friend told me about it, I was smiling because now, that is true giving.

We will talk more about true giving in the last chapter; however, now focus on yourself and your family's responsibility here in the US.

4. Save Money

The tip above explains about prioritizing the important bills you need to pay every month. When you do this, you will need to save for your dreams we also mentioned above. However, there are other things you will need to save for as well.

As a new immigrant, you may be used to the idea of a country offering free post-secondary education. Still, you will soon discover and be shocked that you will need to take a student loan to study for higher education or send your children for college. I know. It was a shock to me too. Although I came from Africa, I didn't have to worry about debt when I went to university to get my bachelor's degree as it was free. Competitive but free.

If you want to go to college to better your life, make sure not to fall into the trap of debt. Instead, look for free resources, scholarships if you have a good GPA, a talent, or are a single parent. There are many scholarships available for different things; find out if you qualify.

There is an option to study online in one of the European universities, as their fees are so low that you could easily afford and pay off in just a few years. Maybe save up for that before you enroll. Recently I was looking at the University of London for a client, and you could get your Masters' program for less than $15,000 vs. in the US; the minimum I have come across was $40,000.

Other areas you might need to save money are for the down payment for buying a house, retirement, down payment for a car, a trip of your dreams, your children's college. You might also want to save for emergencies, for living expenses at least for three months just in case you lose your job or you can't work for whatever reason.

Be frugal, save as much money as you can every month, and watch it accumulate. Which would mean, avoid unnecessary spending. For example, instead of going for "brand" name clothes, look for less expensive clothes. Buy cheaper phones and computers that you can use to achieve your goals, if you go for brands you might have to spend more money, so save the difference.

Another example: don't fall into the trap of eating out just because everyone is doing it in America and because it looks cool. Continue to cook at home, if you don't have time, cook enough for a week on the weekend, and save money instead of eating out all the time.

If you have cable tv, consider eliminating that bill by discontinuing it. You don't have time to watch all the programs you pay for on cable anyways since you are busy building your life. These are just a few examples of how you can save money. Please look for more ways to save more money for your household or hire a financial counselor to help you save money and manage your finances.

5. Spend Money

I know, I know, I just told you to save money, and now I am telling you to spend money, which might be confusing to you.

However, we need to learn a healthier way of managing our savings and spending. Some of us struggle to develop financial rigidity while focusing on saving and might refuse to spend money on important things.

Some immigrants I have met have told me that every time they want to spend money, they mentally convert the American dollar to the currency from their home country, and if it feels too much, they stop themselves from buying something.

They shared with me that when they first arrived in the US, they were used to receiving many free services, and developed a mentality of getting things for free, so they shouldn't spend on important things. However, like I had mentioned earlier when we talked about Government assistance, this kind of mentality will keep you small, and you will not achieve your dreams.

Spend wisely. Save but don't deprive yourself. Cook at home, but treat you and your family or your friends to expensive restaurants once in a while; take your family on a mini-vacation for relaxation because you deserve a reward for the hard work you've been doing. Save, but once in a while, buy one thing on your wish list to reward you and your family for special occasions. Yes, cancel your cable TV to save, but invest in programs like Amazon Prime or Netflix, which costs somewhere like $10 a month, and you can watch movies, and your favorite TV shows, during your down time.

I think you get my point. The purpose of saving is to give you your dream life, the life you came to America for. Saving doesn't need to feel like you are in a prison you can't get out of.

And while we are at it, I want to remind you to spend on yourself when it comes to investing, be it in hiring a coach, buying a book, paying for a class that will advance your knowledge of managing your life in America to be self-reliant. Whatever it is, do it because this kind of spending is adding to your life, and you will save more down the road.

CHAPTER 8

SKILLSET #6: SELF-CONFIDENCE

Webster's dictionary defines self-confidence as *a feeling or consciousness of one's powers or reliance on one's circumstances.* This skillset helps us to take risks, select our choices and decisions. We can't do anything without self-confidence. Whenever we do something, we have to trust in our abilities, qualities, and judgment. Our self-esteem contributes to our self-confidence; it's in one's worth or abilities that creates self-respect in return.

The Oxford dictionary defines self-esteem as *confidence in one's worth or abilities, self-respect.* However, both can build upon each other. It doesn't mean if you are confident you have healthy or high self-esteem. Some people are successful in life; singers, actors, and many others end up ruining their lives using excessive drugs or committing suicide because they have low self-esteem. They don't like or respect themselves. So a person can have self-confidence and low self-esteem.

We build self-esteem and confidence, starting from our childhood: every time we did something right, our parents noticed with approval and clapped for us. We begin building confidence in what we do. I would assume every milestone we hit as kids, crawling, walking, running, jumping, and all these activities develop our self-esteem and confidence.

Growing up, doing good in school, exploring other school curricula like gymnastics, or being good at math, science, drama, sports, soccer game, swimming, whatever we are good at to express ourselves, gave us more confidence, or lack of it, if there was an assumption of failure.

As many things build our self-esteem and self-confidence, many things can crush them and make us fearful in life. Some people with low self-esteem grew up with parents not encouraging them, physical abuse, or sexual abuse, with no one believing in them, so they don't believe in themselves and their abilities as adults. They don't have a good self-image and may not know their worth. It may be challenging to identify people with low self-esteem; these people can be anyone. Their profession doesn't matter; they can be the sweetest or friendliest people you meet, an entertainer, professor at a university, or a doctor.

Self-confidence is the driving strength that helps you live with purpose and achieve your dreams. Self-confidence allows you to feel courageous to go after your dreams because you believe anything is possible.

Confidence isn't like citizenship; once you have it, it doesn't mean you have it forever, and that you don't have to work on it; far from the truth. Our life is ever-evolving, and each time we meet a new situation, circumstances, challenges, we need a new level of confidence. Most of us are confident about something we already know and could feel less satisfied with something new and haven't yet mastered it.

Confidence and crisis

Whenever we meet a new situation, it is normal to feel like we are losing self-confidence. You need to develop a new level of confidence to cope with the recent change, circumstances, and the new you. Of course, if you have healthy self-confidence to begin with, it helps; the process may be faster.

However, sometimes, even if you have self-confidence, some new challenging situations might challenge us to our limits.

I have seen people crack and lose themselves instead of rising to the new level of confidence that they need. Unfortunately, I have met people who committed suicide when something in their life changed, and they thought at that moment, there was no way they could handle it. This feeling is real; it comes to all of us at least once in our life when we're faced with a challenging circumstance that feels like it's beyond our ability.

I have always considered myself a confident person, and in school, I got good grades. When I went to university, I didn't care much for studying because my dream has always been to be a writer, however, I graduated from college.

My confidence has been tested several times in my life. When I gave birth to a special needs child, I had no idea what to do. It was something new, and no one around knew how to handle a special needs child either. All the books I found to read on special needs made me more anxious and depressed because none mentioned what to do for my son, and there wasn't much available where I lived at that time. I felt my self-confidence crumbling and self-doubt crept in. I kept doing what I knew to do while trying to get my son to the Western world to get the services and the equipment he needed to have a life of comfort and meaning.

Once I came to the US, I once again found myself losing my self-confidence because I had no idea how to live in this new culture. It was frustrating that I had to learn everything from scratch. I felt intimidated by the all-knowing Americans. It seemed they knew everything, carefree and didn't care what I thought of them.

However, with time, I began to build my knowledge and confidence.

When the doctor in China told me there was nothing more they could do for my son Aaron, who was two-months-old at the time, and I should hope for the best and prepare for the worse, I was devastated. He told me that my son might never be able to walk or talk. I said to myself: "I don't know how to deal with this information, I don't know how to raise this kind of child," and I didn't know how to stop the enormous pain and loss I was feeling.

If you are reading this book and you find yourself in that pain, please understand that this feeling is temporary, and it will pass. I prayed: "God, I have no idea what I am doing, and I feel so overwhelmed, and I feel sorry for this child that is born to me because I don't know what to do; however, I believe in You, and I trust you to have a grand plan that I don't understand right now. I hate you a bit right now because you are putting me in this situation, and I know all kids are gifts from God, and so please help me, teach me, and show me how to raise this child and how to be a good and strong mom to this child." I have prayed this prayer for many years. I still pray to be the mom that my son needs.

My prayer helped me boost my self-confidence a bit because now my confidence was in a Higher Power, bigger than me, who I believed would help me. Now, when I meet women and men who appreciate me for the kind of mom I am for Aaron and how they respect me, I take that as a confirmation that I have learned to be his mom, no matter how much time it took and how hard and complicated the journey had been.

So if you find yourself in a situation where you have no idea what to do about a crisis you are having, have faith, whatever your belief system is, keep praying, meditate and keep getting up every morning open to learning a new thing. The sadness, the anger, the frustration will be there. Follow some of the tips I gave you on managing your emotions in Chapter 2, and keep going. There will come a day when you look back and realize that although the situation was problematic or challenging, you have developed the confidence needed to handle it.

If you have low self-esteem when you meet your circumstance, having a Higher Power you believe in is so helpful. Because believing that your Higher Power, whether you call that power God, Allah, or the Universe, will give you the confidence you need to meet your circumstances will, in return, build your self-esteem and self-confidence.

Confidence vs. Arrogance

There were times in my life I had no idea what the difference between arrogance and confidence was. Sometimes, I showed arrogance, thinking I was confident. It was an incredible journey for me to transition myself from the road of arrogance to one of confidence. It is why I feel this topic is important.

I meet a lot of immigrants through my work and in my everyday life. I meet people who think they are confident when what they're projecting is pure arrogance. I see it, especially in court, when people are angry and maybe going through a divorce or civil lawsuit. The way they talk to their lawyers, the judges, and the interpreters is not displaying confidence; their behavior rather annoys everyone around them. Yet, in their mind, they are confident. And while the intention is clear, and they want to help their case, their actions show differently.

These people are sure they know what they are doing, trying to convince others of their confidence, and at times it is so embarrassing because everybody else can see they don't know anything. They don't know how to handle their case and are so arrogant they're not open to learning anything new. No one wants to hear a word they say, let alone want to help them.

A family lawyer, who often works with people from my community, once said to me confidentially, "Senait, are all your men arrogant?" I am not mentioning her name, but I knew what she meant, and we had a friendly chat. I explained that they actually think they are demonstrating self-confidence, and it comes off as arrogance. I told her a little background of the culture, which helped her understand where their behavior came from. It's why I included this section in the book because it's important to understand the difference between self-confidence and arrogance.

I have met many clients who have no idea they are arrogant; they think they are confident. It's essential to understand the differences between arrogance and confidence because no one likes to deal with arrogant people. Both arrogant and confident people exhibit a strong belief in their abilities. Those with confidence can easily overcome fears and uncertainty. Moreover, they have a positive and optimistic view that makes them strong and admirable. Sometimes over-confidence turns into arrogance, and it is a significant weakness. Arrogant people usually view themselves as superior and never admit their mistakes. Read on to find out the difference between arrogance and confidence.

After much research on the difference between self-confidence and arrogance, I found six great ways to tell the difference.

1. Condescending remarks

Superiority is the main quality of an arrogant person. Arrogant people are single-minded; they either think that they are superior to others or inferior to them. This arrogance may be nothing more than a way to cover the feelings of inferiority they experience when dealing with someone else. It seems they feel better when they tear others down. On the contrary, confident people are high-minded, because they can feel good without having a desire to offend others. They usually see people's potential and can help them succeed in something.

2. Attitude

Arrogant and confident people treat others differently. An arrogant person thinks they are better than others, while a confident person knows they are just as good as others. Confident people will rarely be found lecturing or preaching to others on how they are wrong. Furthermore, they usually show respect while listening to somebody. Arrogant people have difficulty listening to others. They often exude negative energy and blame others if things do not work out as expected.

3. Self-perception

Confident people always feel comfortable because they have the right conception of perfection. It seems impossible to bring them down because they know their weaknesses and know how to deal with them. Meanwhile, arrogant people brush their shortcomings aside. By virtue of their obstinacy, they cannot admit their mistakes.

4. Relationships With Society

Relationships with arrogant people can be a great source of potential pain. Such people live in their world of self-importance and pride, and nothing affects them. They cannot accept their weaknesses or faults with grace, but blame others for them. A genuinely self-confident person can show vulnerability and even admit past mistakes. Others highly appreciate this quality. By the way, arrogant people can sacrifice friendship or other relationships at the cost of their success.

5. Communication

Communication with arrogant people isn't a pleasant thing. An arrogant person will always try to one-up everything you say. They only mind their position and make others accept their ideas. That's why people try to avoid conversations with them because it's not comfortable to speak with the person who is always right. Confident people don't try to impose their vision of the situation on others. Their accomplishments do it for them.

6. Various Roots

Finally, confidence and arrogance have different origins. Arrogance is usually the result of a defense mechanism used by the subconscious mind to prevent further criticism. Confidence comes from positivity, optimism, and mental steadiness.

Source: https://womanitely.com/ways-difference-arrogant-confident/

If you are like me, you will need to move from arrogance to confidence because no one told you these two roads are different. You probably grew up with people you perceived as confident, who are arrogant instead. You think about your imitation of your mentor's confidence or people you admired growing up, and it might come as a surprise that is not confidence.

Don't worry; awareness is the first step to identify arrogance in your behavior, and it takes little effort to make the shift. Always look at your behavior first to see if you are arrogant or not, instead of looking at people around you. "Hey yeah, this one sounds like my uncle," "Oh my God, this one is exactly like my ex-husband," Although we tend to look at others' faults before we look at ours, let's work at being honest in looking at your behavior first.

A colleague shared with me a story of an arrogant client she dealt with. Instead of directly pointing out to him how arrogant he was, she shared with him a list to tell the difference between being arrogant and being confident for him to connect the dots and maybe see for himself. The next time he saw my colleague, the first thing he said was, "Oh my God! You saved my life; I don't know how to repay you. That list you gave me was amazing. After I read it, I identified all the arrogant people in my life, starting with my ex-wife. Now, I see what the problem was; it was her arrogance."

My colleague and I laughed because he was incapable of looking within himself and projected all the faults on other people. After all, he was right, and they were wrong. Always examine yourself first, and then you will naturally see other people's behavior. But if you focus on others first, you will miss seeing the areas in you that need correction.

After you see yourself, always choose to be confident because everyone wants to associate with people who feel secure and optimistic. If you try to become confident, your relationship skills will be your greatest asset. Have you ever dealt with an arrogant person? Do you want to hang around and be friends with that person? Probably not. Right? You want to be approachable. It will help you find the job you want, build your support system, help you make business connections, and all that.

Now that we know how self-confidence is different from arrogance, let's learn some self-confidence building techniques. We all know when we have confidence and when we don't. When we lack confidence, we feel negative; we criticize ourselves and others, we have negative self-talk about ourselves and our ability. In return, this attitude makes us feel sad, pessimistic, angry, anxious, and even depressed.

There are many reasons why people have low self-confidence. It could be an early life experience, being abused, gender bias, and experiencing racism. But we are not here to analyze why some of us seem to have low self-esteem and high self-confidence. Truth-be-told, we all experience low self-confidence at least once in our lifetime, if not several times.

So let's see how you can build your self-confidence.

Self-confidence is easy to fake. Someone once told me the following when I was at a low point:

1. "Fake it until you make it!"

You can imitate what confident people do. So yeah, practice, and it makes you perfect. Just make sure you imitate a confident person and not an arrogant one.

2. Praying to a higher power helps

Admitting that you are feeling helpless in the face of what is happening around you is helpful. This technique works for me like magic when faced with something beyond my capability. The religion you follow doesn't matter; what you call your Higher Power doesn't matter, turn to who you believe in.

3. Keep looking to the past to see the things you thought you couldn't do or deal with, and now you are doing them correctly, and remember how you felt at that time.

This tool always makes me smile, and I say to myself, "it's like before; once I learn this new thing or know how to deal with it, everything will be great! I have done it before, and I can do it again." This attitude automatically brings out your confidence.

If you are feeling less confident because of a new thing you don't know, educate yourself. Read books on it, or enroll in a class. It will boost your confidence level.

At this time, I have low confidence in speaking Italian with my in-laws. Although I know so many words, every time I talk to them, I feel embarrassed. To boost my confidence, I bought books and CD's to help me study more. I watch cartoons in Italian with my son Joseph, so next time I visit my Italian in-laws, I will feel like my confidence level is rising to at least communicate with what I know, and that in return will give me the confidence to learn more.

4. Positive self-talk

It helps to talk positively to yourself.

Even though I have always been a writer (I have to tell you I kept diaries through my most difficult times, it's therapy to me), writing to publish is next-level for me. While writing this book, every once in a while, self-doubt would creep in, and I would hear negative self-talk: "who do you think you are? It isn't good enough. What do you think you are doing?" It's interesting; usually, I would laugh it off and shake it off. However, when writing this section about self-confidence, I found myself paralyzed for a few days. I couldn't write anything, and I felt like I was wasting my time doing other things when I was supposed to write. I remembered what a close relative said to me several times in anger, "you are nothing, you are never going to amount to anything, you are nobody, and you will never be anybody."

I realized I was feeling paralyzed in writing this section because my relative's voice kept repeating in my mind, and it was so depressing, I teared up. I told my husband about it, and he helped me by asking me questions like, "Is that true? Do you believe he is right? Do you believe you are nothing and that you are a nobody?" I said immediately, "of course not!" As soon as I replied, I felt better. I spent the whole day doing some positive self-talk, countering the voice in my head that I didn't even know was living in my subconscious.

I have reasoned with myself how that relative was a self-destructive person, which was his way of controlling people. He had no self-confidence and would always put people down by being mean and rude to others to attempt to show his false inner power.

I made a list of the reasons why I was the right person to write this book. Yes, I know others might write better than me. Yes, English is not my first language. However, no one can write this book the way I can because it's my story, my book, and my perspective. We are all unique, and it's my self-expression, and nobody could write this book better than me. Writing doesn't know any boundaries, including language. English might not be my first language, but I speak and write well, and when I make mistakes, an editor can help me and enhance my writing.

That was it! I was back on the wagon again. I felt refreshed getting back to writing. My self-talk and positive talk with my husband boosted my self-confidence back to where I needed it.

When encountering a new adventure, whether it's a new business, writing a book, traveling to a new country, starting a new job, competing in the Olympics, getting married, or starting a family, understand that the first enemy you will face is yourself, your thoughts. It's true for everyone. It will attack, try to put you down, and convince you to change your mind. So, every time you feel defeated by your inner critic, prepare counter self-talk to keep you on track. Be gentle and compassionate towards yourself. Once you master how to silence your inner critic, you will know how to overcome the outside critic.

5. Talk to Friends You Trust

My friends know me well, and whenever I tell them I am feeling less confident about something, they jump in and help boost my confidence by reminding me of who I am, where I have been, and what I'm capable of doing.

Because no matter how strong and confident we are, there are circumstances that throw us off, and at that time, a good friend you trust and has your best interest in their heart can lift you like no other.

When you're feeling insecure around others about your language, or don't know the culture, remember that the people might not even know how to speak a second language. They appreciate how you are trying to learn their language while speaking one or more of your native languages. English isn't your first language, and you are making an effort to learn to master it. How cool is that? Only confident people are willing to learn something new to improve their lives. So don't sell yourself short. You are one of the few brave people who went beyond normal to make their lives better.

I am sure there are millions of ways to build your confidence, and I encourage you to read more on this topic if you think you have less self-confidence in one or more parts of your life. The above tools I mentioned are a few that work for me in my life. You can adopt them or create your own.

Confidence and Racism

What is racism? It is prejudice, discrimination, or antagonism directed against someone of a different race based on the belief that one's own race is superior.

It's one thing to be confident when things are working your way, and it's completely different when things are against you. You will face many things in the US that you have never seen before. like racism. (You will also face discrimination like you are use to, like gender discrimination.) However, none test your self-confidence like racism does. It blinds, doesn't make sense, annoying, triggers your anger, and sometimes you might even feel self-diminished.

I remember my first encounter with racism; I was in China in my late twenties. It was the first place I went outside of my continent, Africa. Before coming to China, I only heard about racism at school while learning about Black History in America. I watched a few American movies that gave me some idea of racism.

When I arrived in China, I had no idea how others perceived me. Some were curious about me; some were rude and even scary in the way they stared or abruptly touched me to feel my skin. Since I had never experienced racism because of my color, nor had I ever been at the center of attention because I was different, I didn't know what to do except being upset and wanting to leave their country as soon as possible.

Then I met a few African friends that helped me through the process. They helped me get through the tough times of adjusting to racism. I realized not all people in China were racist. I learned that some Chinese cities were more adjusted to other ethnicities, and I wouldn't even feel it. The people in Dalian, the city where I lived, were not accustomed to seeing foreigners at that time, especially Black people, so they were curious. Sometimes, too curious to the point of a stranger touching my hand to feel my skin was very rude and annoying to me. I have had many incidents in which strangers touched me and tried to rub my skin off. Strangers were asking me if I took a shower every day, grabbed my hand, talked to their friend in Mandarin while rubbing my skin, paying no attention to me as if I was a toy. I felt like an animal in a zoo. It was a horrifying experience, and I have many stories I could share; however, I will move on.

You can imagine my terror in approaching people, and I wanted to go back to Africa, where I was not different. However, I soon started teaching English, and I was hanging out with kids a lot! Kids are innocent and give you a perspective into the culture you wouldn't otherwise have. I love kids in any culture because they are uncensored, and they say whatever comes to their minds. While teaching them, they raised many questions that they were curious about, like why I was black and why I have big eyes (they liked my big eyes). Because it was coming from kids, I didn't feel offended; I was more focused on finding ways to answer their questions in a way they would understand. My students and I found a way around their curiosity. Because they were innocent with their questions, and I was open to innocently looking for answers.

I previously told you about my friend who asked me if I took showers. I saw the whole culture as one big curious culture because their borders have been closed for so long they never knew how to interact with foreigners at that time, especially Black. They didn't know anything about personal boundaries or how their reaction could terrorize me. They were acting at a moment of wonder.

I started making friends, and then I found out like every culture, some are curious, some lack knowledge about the topic of racism and other cultures, and yet, some were darn racist. They wouldn't change their minds even if you put information before them because they have decided that they are superior to a darker race.

It was an adventure. I learned a lot about myself and the Chinese culture. I learned to love the country, and way of life. I impacted the children I was teaching. I was influenced and changed by my students and the culture in general. Most of the time, it was overwhelming and stressful to be looked at differently. I sometimes wanted to run away, hide, throw stones at people, lash out in anger, and ask them what they were looking at.

Had I gone back home initially, after being overwhelmed in the beginning, I wouldn't have understood the rich culture. I wouldn't have met those amazing students who have changed my life forever as I have changed theirs; I wouldn't have gotten to know the people I have met, the friends I made, and I wouldn't have had the rich experience I gained that money can't buy. I am forever grateful for sticking around for two years and learning to discover myself as a Black person living among non-Black people, a Black person with confidence.

Then I moved to the USA, and that was a different experience for me. Back then, racism was not openly expressed in the US as frequently as it is now. I was faced with subtle racism every day that was, at times, so hard to detect. It was so annoying to me because even if I spotted racism, it would be so subtle that the other person could deny it. Racism was a taboo for so long in the USA, people and institutions found a subtle way to keep perpetuating it. It was so difficult to know if someone was just curious or actually being racist. I experienced some white women asking if they could touch my hair, as they never interacted with a black woman before. Sometimes, when I kept my black hair natural, some people would stare at me funny at workplaces, something that made me uneasy. Once, I was called "Nigger" by a white woman who was mad at me. I have been refused services, treated unfairly, and ignored. I also experienced racism within the Black community; it was so frustrating to navigate it all.

After Trump became President, people seemed to have found permission to be openly racist since he is openly racist. One common experience of most immigrants is the racist comment, "go back to your country." I have never had that said to my face; however, I have had my clients go through it, and I have often seen the same sentence written by angry people on social media. It can make you feel angry, frustrated, afraid, and betrayed. It could feel like the USA promised us the American dream, but they didn't say anything about racism. Acknowledge that there is racism in America and that it has a long history; since you are now part of that story, you are about to learn how to live as a person of color in the USA. A confident person of color in the USA who achieves their dream no matter the obstacles.

Tools on Confidence and Racism

1. In every culture, you will meet racist people; they may accept and love you. Some will misunderstand you; some will want to know you, some will be curious and don't know how to approach you, and may act weird. Some

might ignore you because they don't know anything about your culture or where you are from: they don't want to sound stupid. I said in every culture, which means even the country you left. Understanding this fact will liberate you. Don't take it personally. That is how people are everywhere you travel. Drop the idea that everyone is a racist like I first did when I arrived in China. Some people are just so curious and might act strangely, but they don't necessarily think they are superior to you because of their color or other factors. So, don't label everyone as racist.

2. Identify the people around you. Now that you live in the US, you will meet all kinds of people, and it's challenging to see racism unless it is relatively apparent. Mostly racism is subtle. Some people even might hide it very well because the law protects people from discrimination, and people have gotten good at hiding it. Observe the people: your friend who isn't from your country, your boss, your colleagues. Observe what they say and how they treat other people and see if they treat you the same. Subtle racism is hard to spot: you might feel that something is not right in a group of your friends, but you can't put your finger on it. Through time you'll be good at spotting it. Read more about racism. With our past president Donald Trump saying racist things, people are showing their honest thoughts about racism more openly with the current

political situation. Although I don't support Trump nor racism, I like things to be in the open, and the current situation has the merit of exposing racism more openly, so you may know how people feel about you.

3. Understand and know you can't change the people that will always think they are superior to you no matter what you do. Know this fact and stop getting upset, mad, and refrain from teaching the person or confronting them. They are not worth your time, and it's not your job to change or fix people. You will only get frustrated and depressed. Please stay away from these people because they will try to affect your self-confidence and make you doubt yourself. Know it isn't about you; it's their issue, and you don't have to put yourself at their level.

4. Know that racism exists in all cultures and towards all kinds of people. Look in your region of origin. Does one ethnic group or area feel superior to the other and mistreat people for that? It might or might not be for the skin color, but it's racism, nonetheless. In my culture, we have nine ethnic groups. Some groups are light-skinned, while some are darker, and I have seen and heard people discriminate and make racist comments. There are still parents who refuse to let their children marry outside of their village, their region, even if the people living in the area next to them are of the same Ethnic group. You can see this in the whole of Africa if you look closer. And

when asked why they don't allow these marriages; they will tell you they don't mix their blood with inferior blood. Imagine racism exists even if we are all black.

However, please know that I am not excusing racism in America. I am merely letting you know that it isn't anything new when you experience racism in the US, although the weight becomes heavier because you are in a foreign country. You are dealing with people outside of your country and community. Understanding this will help you see human beings' dysfunctional nature trying to discriminate against people and thinking one race is superior makes them feel good about themselves.

The worst history of racism is what brought World War II. The Nazis thought that the white race was superior to other races, which served as a justification for the mistreatment and massacre of the Jews. The Nazis didn't think the Jews were white enough.

Think also about the slave trade that mistreated Africans by depriving them of their dignity, sold them, treated them like animals, and made them labor for free to enrich others.

How horrifying is that? And to make matters worse, instead of getting an apology for slavery and getting acknowledged for being the backbone of America's economy, African Americans continued to be oppressed by the American system for generations. That is part of our human history.

Even if overall it's getting better, we still struggle with racism and discrimination worldwide. So, every time you face racism, know you are not singled out; you are not alone; at some point, it happens to everyone in a lifetime. It doesn't make it right, but be part of the solution by being confident despite that and accomplish your purpose with dignity. Know that it isn't about who you are or where you are from, but it's about the other person's limited way of thinking. I recommend that you feel sorry for them, have compassion, avoid them, and move on. It doesn't mean we ignore racism and discrimination, but you being upset and letting this affect your self-confidence isn't worth it. There are other ways to advocate and fight for the cause in which you believe.

5. Identify and know your rights! I hate to admit this, but racism and discrimination don't only exist with your friends, neighbors, or strangers; it also lies with institutions and maybe even governmental places. Knowing your rights will help you be confident to say something about it when it happens. It could happen when you try to rent an apartment, buy something, or go somewhere special. Talk to a lawyer; if you know your rights are being violated, you can tell the person what you

are seeing and know your rights, and you will take this to their supervisors.

The US law doesn't tolerate racism and discrimination because of color, sexual orientation, gender, disability, and many more. Knowing your rights will give you confidence and prevent others from mistreating you and help you not waste your time being angry and shouting, but learn to advocate for yourself and your family.

6. Since the killing of George Floyd by a police officer and protests proliferated in the US, people in the USA and worldwide are paying attention. There are social movements like Black Lives Matter that advocate against police brutality incidents and all racially motivated violence against black people. White people are having conversations about this issue in the US, as well.

   While people have a global conversation about racism, some people talk about it peacefully, but you might also see those who resist and say there is no racism; they don't want to admit such a thing exists. However, I believe having it in the open, with people worldwide discussing it, is a good thing, and it's good to be part of the dialog.

You can talk about your experience of racism, and you should also teach your kids about racism so that if it happens to them, they will feel prepared.

However, no matter what you do, don't be the person who thinks he/she can't get ahead in life because people in this country are racist. Yes, some people in this country are still racist, but it didn't prevent other Black or people of color from succeeding in life. So, don't use it as an excuse not to pursue your dreams and achieve those dreams despite the challenge of racism. When you do, you have already become an example for other people of color and immigrants to do the same. So, you fight and defeat racism by being positive and being focused on your goals and achieving them, having a dialog with others, and being part of the global discussion.

Confidence and life challenging circumstances

As I said before, life circumstances bring us to our knees, and some lower our self-confidence. Such as, your child gets sick and you don't know what to do, divorce, family or friends betrayal, a loved one's death, losing your job you are good at, being rejected by someone or at work, a miscarriage, and other things that might challenge our confidence. We all go through it.

How can you trust yourself to be in a relationship again after a divorce? You thought it was the right relationship, and it didn't work out. Many people never remarry and choose to suffer in loneliness because they are afraid to try again, as they have lost their self-confidence when it comes to marriage. I know two people that have been in a car accident and never want to drive a car again. They chose to use public transportation and other means because they could never trust themselves to drive again. They lost their self-confidence.

I know people who swear they will never make friends again because friends betrayed them in the past. We all face a setback in self-confidence after facing a difficult circumstance.

My most significant loss of self-confidence was having another baby after going through a very traumatic experience with my first son's birth and the complications. It took me ten years to consider having another child. People around me didn't see it as a loss of self-confidence because they could see I was confident in other areas of my life.

I also hid it so well from myself for a long time. I unconsciously made sure not to have another child by not creating the situation for it to happen. I avoided serious relationships. For example, I was like a repellent for anyone who wanted to get serious with me for a long time. I couldn't get past a certain point in a relationship. Yes, we can even hide things from ourselves. It is possible to have confidence in one area of your life and not in another.

Although this process is a normal reaction, we need to regain our confidence to have a fulfilling life. We must strive to forgive ourselves (and others) and try again.

Here are some tips on how you can do that:

1. Identify where you have lost confidence in your life. Look into the area of your life that you are struggling with or complain about a lot. Your friendships? Your career? Your love life? Your marriage? You want to change something in that area, but for whatever reason, you can't? You feel stuck. You can't take action.

To use the previous example again, I couldn't figure out why my relationship with men didn't work past a certain point. When people asked me why I wasn't remarrying, I told them I didn't know. At some point, I believed I was not the marrying kind; I used to think: "I don't want to, I have no time, I am busy with my son."

When I further examined the issue, I realized I wanted to be in a healthy relationship and have more kids, but fear stopped me. I finally found two causes: I didn't want to get hurt, and I was terrified of having another child. Being serious in a relationship and or getting married meant putting myself in front of a possible heartache and pregnancy.

So unconsciously, I had put a big wall around my heart that no man could penetrate. But I disguised it by saying to myself that marriage was not for me. Those were excuses, hiding my two worst fears that were keeping me lonely and safe. Most of all, I lost self-confidence in trusting myself to choose the right partner and giving birth to a healthy child.

Look in your life and find the area you are struggling with; keep thinking, pray, if you believe, and find out the underlying fear you are trying to cover. Be very truthful with yourself. You don't have to share this with anyone unless you feel comfortable. It's between you and your God.

2. Once you find the area, start the healing process. Different methods and therapy can help you, such as family, health therapists, and grief counselors. Talk to your doctor and ask them to refer you to

a therapist to help with specific issues. Once you have done the inner work of healing your past or wound, whatever that is, and whatever time it takes, you will feel your self-confidence coming back slowly in that area you have been struggling with.

If you find two or more areas of your life where you have lost your confidence and sense of power, take one area first and take baby steps to heal yourself and recover your self-confidence.

Move to the next area you want to work on after you have succeeded in the first area. After the first one, it becomes natural, you will get used to the process, and you may be able to do it yourself.

After I found the truth about why I wasn't marrying again and the fear and loss of confidence in that area, I went to a counselor who helped me find ways to release my fear and develop good positive self-talk. I talked to my good friends, who encouraged me, which started to build my self-confidence again. I prayed and meditated a lot. And like magic, my heart healed, and after a few years of the process, I got the confidence to date the man I married. He is a wonderful man, and we now have two other healthy boys: Joseph and Michael, who bring happiness and joy to our family.

When using any of the tools I listed above, if you feel overwhelmed with emotions that last for days, if you feel like crying all the time and depressed, these are warning signs that you may need a mental health professional to help you get through it. Remember, you should consider the mental professional as a partner, not someone you should fear. Seeing a mental health professional doesn't mean you are crazy; it's the opposite. You are smart enough to seek help to heal yourself.

In conclusion, self-confidence is like a plant; it goes through cycles. It needs nurturing and attention, and it grows with experience and age. Sometimes we feel confident about something; other times, we feel less secure, which is expected, as long as we don't get stuck in it. Like plants, we are supposed to go through cycles, but our self-confidence should keep growing and not regress. Keep on working on your self-confidence in all stages of your life. Please read about it, educate yourself, and talk with your friends. And with your ever-growing self-confidence, you will be able to get that job you wanted and the life that you've always dreamed of.

CHAPTER 9

SKILLSET #7: THE DANCE OF CULTURAL INTEGRATION

Now that you know the steps that can help you in your journey to navigate cultural integration and make it easier, let's make sure you don't fall from the wagon while building all these healthy habits and steps you are learning.

Learning something new is not easy. Sometimes, we can only learn one skill at a time. Even multiple times, but it needs to be consistent. Repetition makes perfect. It's like building a muscle. Learning new things can be painful, and you need to keep your body, mind, and spirit healthy to keep learning.

Keeping yourself healthy

One thing that will help with this is healthy food. If you have come from a developing country as I did, you will face a culture shock with the foods you eat, because they are not like you are used to. You will be confused at first: why does everyone seem to talk about food and is obsessed with their weight?

You will hear so many suggestions and methods on how you eat and what you should eat that it can be confusing and overwhelming. At times you might find it so hard to know what to eat and what to avoid. You probably never faced this kind of problem before. You ate organic because no other type of processed food was available to you in your country of origin. Now since you came to the US, you can't understand your body anymore.

I have met many clients that fear eating. And starve themselves because they don't know what they were hearing about the food being not organic and not healthy. They develop a lot of anxiety not knowing what to eat and how to make sense of all the confusing methods presented to them.

Even people born and raised in the States get confused about the conflicting information. Many people born in the US whom I interviewed told me they had tried all the plans out there before settling to a diet that they feel comfortable with. Some people I interviewed said they prefer to eat out because they don't have to cook at home and this saves them time. So I know many families that go out both for lunch and dinner with their families daily. They are so busy at work up till the evenings. It is another culture shock for many of us.

Nowadays, though, I see many people becoming conscious about their food, and there are many people encouraging others to cook at home. There is also a vegan movement on the rise, asking for a change in the amount of meat Americans consume.

It's good to educate yourself with different diet methods. However, the most effective that I found for me is working out your system of eating. Like everybody else, I also went through all the confusion of different diets and programs. I tried some of them, read a lot about diet, and finally came up with what works for me and me only.

You know yourself; you don't have to stick to some plan just because everyone you know is doing that. You want to find what works for you, and as long as the goal is healthy eating, you get to make your own choice about how you and your family stay healthy. Of course, the first thing you might want to do is talk to your doctor. Tell your doctor what you like to eat, and you want to eat healthy food. Ask what you should do or what plan you should follow. That always helps. But sometimes, doctors also don't want to give a lot of advice because that might look like trying to sell you to something (as some doctors might do). But mostly, doctors will be honest with you and tell you what you need to hear.

As for me, one of my biggest culture shocks was (and still is) to see how people in the US (and western countries in general) are obsessed with food and their weight. I know it might seem hard not to feel this massive pressure from the culture you live in, but try not to be dragged into it. Stay in your lane. Find a way to eat healthily and exercise regularly, and you will be fine. The culture I come from follows a fasting season; all religions have their fasting seasons, although they might be different. My mom follows an orthodox Christian religion. I was never a follower of their practice, like fasting or any other rules, as I am not a religious person, but deeply spiritual. However, recently I got curious, and after really looking into it, I decided to study how they fast and their meaning. It made perfect sense to me, and I decided to follow that fasting system throughout the year. Sometimes, what you are looking for is right in front of you, already included in your home country's traditions, and you don't need to look for some expensive diet plan, which would also result in frustration.

I am not a nutritionist, and this isn't advertising for any sale nor advising for religion. I'm sharing what works for me after a lot of struggle. However, you are welcome to copy what I do if you can't develop your plan or take inspiration on how to determine and design your method.

The Orthodox diet is fascinating; they fast for 180 days in a year. And when I say "fasting" in this case, it means refraining from any animal products: you eat nothing but vegan food during the fasting period. The days and months are spread out throughout the year and the longest you fast continuously is 55 days. This system works for me perfectly, as I don't want to overeat meat since I grew up mostly vegetarian, but I also don't want to give up meat because I believe it is essential for my body.

My husband and I also cook at home. We have a busy life but eating healthy is always on top of our priorities: we eat at home or pack our lunches, with occasional date nights eating out. And on the date that I go out with my husband or friends, I don't eat salad. I spoil myself with any food I want. I also eat fast food without feeling guilty or ashamed because I don't eat fast food daily. I also use intermittent fasting when I need to.

I started growing my vegetables in our backyard a year ago, and we eat some vegetables out of our garden. I am still learning and planting more: my goal is to get good at it and get at least 95% of my vegetables from the garden. And I am learning my best to accomplish that dream.

I feel comfortable with this method when it comes to healthy eating. You want to avoid processed food as much as possible as it is where most unhealthy calories and other stuff you don't want to eat come from. No matter what method you use, try to eat fresh. Thank God for technology, cooking isn't difficult any more even if you don't know how to cook, look on YouTube for cooking videos.

The goal should always be about being healthy, not on losing weight. Because it tends to frustrate everyone, however, it's also what everyone talks and worries about. If you focus on eating healthy and maintaining a healthy lifestyle, you don't need to worry about anything.

Exercise

When I first moved to the US, another culture shock was the health and weight exercise advertisements. Growing up accustomed to eating organic food, I was also used to moving around in the small city by public transportation and bicycle. I used to take my bike to school and even to work most of the time. I drove a car and loved it, but usually limited to social occasions. I guess that is one of the advantages of living in a small city.

After coming to the US, I noticed that I was spending most of my day driving or sitting, and the lifestyle didn't support any movement. I finally understood the need for many gyms and exercise places scattered throughout the city. People have to make a special stop at the gym to move their bodies.

I have to admit, I indeed saw the benefit and tried different gyms, boot camp programs, Tai Chi, and Yoga programs. Going through the process gave me the experience to learn a lot about myself. I realized that I didn't need gyms and structured classes to move my body. I loved the idea of moving my body throughout the day effortlessly, so I designed my exercise routine.

Moving your body is essential, and gyms and other institutions are there to support that. However, don't forget they are in business to make money, and yes, they are making money helping people to move their bodies to maintain their health. I have much respect for these businesses, and if you like classes and gyms, I suggest you research them and sign-up for the one that best fits your needs or interests. If not, let's combine both and find a way to keep your body moving.

1. Make a list of the things you like, hobbies, and
    things that involve movement, such as hiking,

dancing, Tai Chi, and riding a bike. Now that you have listed the activities you love to do, see where you can fit them in your days, before/after work, or the weekend.

2. Make time for movement and activities with friends. You can challenge your friends, create an exercise routine that you can do together, or report to each other by phone, online, or other digital platforms where you can share how your exercise was. It's an excellent opportunity for your friends to hold you accountable for your workout, and they can do the same for you.

Some examples to keep your body moving:
- Use public transportation
- Ride your bike (in the US, there are special parking spots for your bikes)
- Take the stairs instead of elevators
- If you're busy with very young kids, go for a stroller walk
- Walk during your lunch break
- Walk in the evening after you put your kids to sleep or before you retire to a good night sleep

There are many ways you could squeeze in movement. It should come naturally, not forced. Remember, the goal should be to maintain a healthy lifestyle.

Focus

We can't do anything without focus. The western world will require you to be a master in keeping your attention. Before coming to the US, I never had trouble focusing because what I was doing was limited and predictable daily. I never had stress related to work or my everyday life. I went to school and studied; I might have experienced stress and anxiety when it came to exams. Simple societies usually have simple lives. It's generally working, school, family gatherings for meals, meet friends, read a good book, or go out with friends, and repeat the cycle. Sometimes when I feel overwhelmed by western life, I briefly wish I were back into the simple lifestyle once again.

Coming to the US, life takes a different turn. Everything around you is designed to distract you from your goals and attention. Sometimes it can be overwhelming. The TV, food, advertisement, smartphones, marketing emails... a hundred gazillion things are going on around you that are distractions. It makes focusing on what you are trying to accomplish extremely difficult. Our goal is to stay focused in the face of distractions, and it requires practice.

- To practice, we need to minimize our distractions. Make time for your smartphone; you don't have to feel obligated to answer your phone every time it rings unless it's an emergency. Let it go to voicemail. Put your phone on silent while working on an important task. Turn off notifications. You can return the phone calls when you're available.

- The internet is one of the biggest distractions, including social media.

These days I let go of the internet much faster than I used to. Before, while I was "surfing" the internet, I would notice receiving an email, and I would feel like I had to reply; then I would see a message I received on my Facebook. I would get distracted to the point of forgetting what I was doing. With practice, I have become much better at going on the internet and doing what I'm supposed to do without distractions.

Mastering this skill of keeping focus in the face of distractions is very important for your productivity and whatever you are doing. If you have kids, know that they are also continually distracted by their surroundings. If you haven't mastered how to stay focused on what you set out to do, you won't be able to mentor and guide your kids to be focused when they are not.

Tips for Writing Your Goals

1. Write down your goals nightly and put the tasks on your calendar that must be done for that specific day and at what time. It helps you focus and will remind you what you need to do when the day goes by.

   This practice requires discipline on your part daily. Some days you will do everything on your calendar, sometimes not, but keep practicing: you will be great at it before you know it. And don't strive to be perfect; be efficient. No one is perfect. Expect sometimes to fail and feel distracted that you're not able to accomplish anything as you planned. It's ok, as long as you keep practicing. Get up the next morning and try again.

2. Write down what you want to accomplish every month and year. That way, you have your work cut out for you. It will give you the structure of what to achieve at certain times and not aimlessly wander. It's important. What we see every day is overwhelming; people will try to hook you up to what they are doing. If you don't have a direction of where you are going, you will be distracted by whoever crosses your path and end up doing what they want to do instead.

However, if you have written goals that you have set to accomplish every month and year, you know what you will be working on every week to achieve your goals. It's also essential to go back and look at your progress. If you have more things on your list that you didn't do, you have more than likely been distracted by other items, not on your list.

If this happens to you, don't beat yourself up, this process helps you to self-evaluate how focused you are each month. Some months, you may be super attentive, and some you may be less focused. Just keep doing it; through time, you will make a lot of progress. So keep writing your goals for a year, then break them down by month, weeks, and finally, days. This exercise will help you focus on what is essential in your life and prioritize your goals over distractions when the temptations come.

Being patient with yourself is necessary. You may fail many times before you get a hold of this system. We are human, and learning takes time.

3. They say exercising, eating healthy, and sleeping enough hours also contribute to being focused on what you do the whole day. So keep at it! Treat your body like a Mercedes Benz, add good food, move it around, and give it the rest it deserves.

I have shared above what helps me to focus the most. You may adapt and read books to maximize your focus because we can't accomplish our goals without focus.

Mastering Survival

Know when to switch from "always to live in survival mode." It becomes apparent when you realize you are no longer worried about some things that used to worry you: you have food on your table every day, you're able to pay rent and bills, and you can start saving. Once you reach this stage, it feels good, and you know you are ready for the next stage and next step in your financial freedom. However, there is a fear that comes with that, you want to hold onto what you have, and it's normal to want to stay where you are not to lose what you have accomplished so far. Sometimes, our brains get traumatized when we lose everything and have to rebuild from zero; we, therefore, try to make sure that it doesn't happen again.

The trick is to have trust in the higher power and yourself; after all, you have made it to where you are now because of your hard work, prayers, good judgment, government assistance, and determination to have your life together. Remember to build your self-confidence to move to new ventures.

Like I said in a previous chapter, wanting to go to the next stage might require you to give up your government assistance if you have any.

For example, let's say you found a job that pays you good money; however, taking it means you might have to give up your financial assistance. When this happens, trust and take the job, give up the government assistance and see what happens. You will surprise yourself for sure. And if, for some reason, the job you got doesn't work out and you find yourself needing assistance from the government, you can always apply again. However, if you don't try, you will never know what you are capable of.

However, some of the next steps might require you to keep your government assistance. For example, you might decide to go back to school so you can earn more.

In this case, it's ok to keep receiving government assistance to focus on your studies. Once you are finished with your studies, graduate, and find a job, you can take the next step to free yourself of government assistance.

If you don't push your potential, you can't grow and live abundantly with freedom of mind. If instead you try to get more money by doing jobs under the table, because you are afraid of losing government assistance, you will expose yourself to trouble.

And furthermore:

1. You will never find out how powerful you can be by doing more and becoming more of who you always wanted to be.

2. If you choose to do something illegal, you risk your safety, and you will be putting your family in jeopardy.

3. To keep receiving government assistance when your income exceeds the standard is fraud. Even if the government doesn't discover what you have been doing, you might lose sleep because you're worried about being discovered. Your mind works better when it's not cluttered with worries. Besides, didn't you come to the US for freedom? That instead sounds like prison.

4. If you have kids, you know that they learn by observing and not by what you say. If you are hiding your potential, your kids automatically learn to hide theirs as well. You might say no, "but I daily encourage my kids to study to be better than me." I hear the same from a lot of my clients. Sorry, but it doesn't work that way, your kids will be what they observe, and they will learn not to push for their full potential if that is what they see. If we want our kids to be hardworking, independent, and fierce in

pursuing their dreams, we need to show them how to
walk what we preach to them.

A few years ago, I heard of an African immigrant lady who worked as
a custodian at a hospital until all her kids graduated from college. She
never missed a day of work, and was recognized for her many years of
hard work. Her kids all have successful careers now, and when I saw
them talk about their mom I felt so touched and inspired. They were
trying to persuade their mom to retire since they all graduated. In an
interview, one of her daughters said, "My mom showed me what hard
work means." What a powerful story! It brought me to tears.

Some immigrants worry that their kids may end up being drug
addicts and criminals because of being tempted by the way of life in
America. This single mother focused on demonstrating to her kids
what it means to be a hardworking human being even if you don't have
enough education.

Although we may be tempted to blame America for how some
immigrant children turn out as adults, sometimes it's how we live
our lives that has the most influence on a destructive lifestyle.
Yes, I know. That is a hard pill to swallow, and we might not want
to hear it.

When we demonstrate our best selves, work hard in whatever
field, and show our kids what it means to go after their dreams, they
will automatically learn to do the same and strive to be like us. When
you tell them to keep working hard, they will listen because you are a
perfect example for them. Let's not tell our kids what they need to do

or be; let's be an example and show them how it's done. It's human nature to point fingers and blame others, "It's the government's fault; it's the culture's fault." However, the people we talk about were raised at home. Everything starts at home. We must take responsibility for our part. It doesn't mean everything on the outside is perfect. No. Far from it! However, when we see something wrong, for example, racism or our rights being violated, show your kids how you handle the situation with grace. They can learn from you what to do to advocate for their rights. When you react negatively and say things like, "People are so racist in this country," complaining about how your rights are always violated, and no one cares. It is what your kids learn to do. So let's be our best selves, educate ourselves on our rights, and let's live by example, not by telling.

Sadly, some immigrants feel overwhelmed, decide they can't do anything about what is happening around them, and turn to ease their pain and frustration in the wrong way. They turn to alcohol, addictions, divorce, abuse, overworking, and displaying unhealthy behavior at home. Kids exposed to these behaviors may make the same choices.

I met an immigrant dad once who was an alcoholic, and he told me, "I have good behaviors too, but my 21-year-old son takes after my bad behavior, how is that possible?" Some studies show that if a child sees destructive behaviors at home, he will likely default to the same. It's important to fix our family's brokenness for our children to thrive in our society.

The above examples are extreme cases, but kids learn everything from you by observation, not by what you say. My dad once caught me smoking when I was 17. He was heartbroken and gave me the same speech of the father from the previous example, "You picked up the one bad habit that I have that I didn't want you to, instead of getting the good things from me."

He was right; I started smoking, which isn't appropriate in the culture I came from, but I started because I thought it was cool. I thought my dad was cool when he smoked. It took many heartaches, money, and energy to quit and understand that smoking isn't cool. It was a destructive habit.

To teach our kids good manners and be independent and confident, we have to demonstrate those skills, which is why we have to continually learn and improve throughout our lives and never hide our potential.

We must be our unique selves, strive and go for our dreams; our children will learn from what they observe. Our kids don't care about the kind of job we have; they care how hard we work and how we strive to go to the next level. We can't teach our kids to be independent unless we show them how to be independent.

Life isn't perfect and doesn't always go the way we want. If we have done everything in our power, but our children turn out to be somehow not the way we wanted them to be, then we wouldn't blame ourselves for the way they turned out because we have done everything we know to do and we have set an example. If we haven't done our best to be our best, the guilt will be hard on us.

Your potential is untapped, and you have no idea how powerful you are and how successful you can be. So don't be afraid to take a leap of faith. If you fall, you are now an expert in looking for resources to find help.

That is the beauty of being in the USA. We have resources and assistance you might not find anywhere else.

Meet the New You

The more you integrate successfully into your new country, the more you feel like you don't recognize yourself. People will say you have changed. Some people might even try and shame you if you don't fit into how they think you should behave.

Don't worry. You are becoming the new you! If you have been integrating the right way, you will see someone who is, at the same time, from the country of origin and the new country when you look at yourself. You have one leg in the culture you left and the other leg in the US culture. It means you have picked up what is good in the US culture and ignored the bad; at the same time, you have taken your values and what you cherish from your culture of origin and left behind what no longer serves you.

If you ever have to go back to your country of origin, don't worry about the skills or values you seemed to have lost while living in the USA; in that case, it will all come back to your mind, like riding a bicycle.

Meet the new you! This incredible person is rich in perspective from both the culture you grew up in and the culture you are integrating into. You can see the US culture with different eyes than the people who have lived here for years; you will see the potential, the problems, and you might even see the solutions.

On the other hand, you will look at the culture you left behind in a new way too, and you may be ready to contribute in a more significant way when the time comes. Why? Because you are a leader.

Leadership/What is Next?

What's next is your leadership in giving back. Giving back has nothing to do with having a lot of money. It is an attitude. Most of us feel and think, "I will start giving when I have more time or when I have enough of this and that."

However, if you don't have a giving nature, you will not magically start to give when you get wealthy or become a millionaire.

The attitude of giving starts with curiosity and with asking yourself, "How may I serve?" This attitude will help you with your family, friends, marriage, and community.

Giving is fulfilling. There is nothing wrong with receiving, but the beauty of life is when you give and take and when the balance is maintained. Of course, when you newly emigrate, no one should expect you to give back in any way. Everything you have is being invested in getting your life together. It's ok; don't feel guilty about not giving back.

However, even if you are new to the USA and are struggling, you can think, at least once a day, "How can I serve?" Keep asking yourself that even if you don't know how you can. And I am sure the answer will come to you. Maybe you will feel to volunteer at the church/mosque you go to, if you go to a house of prayer. If not, perhaps you have a child that goes to school, and you will see an opportunity to volunteer there. It could be helping someone with their grocery bags at the store as long as you ask politely.

When you first came to the US, perhaps you might have gone to a food bank and received monthly donations; you can now volunteer at the place that helped you. You can donate your kid's clothes or your clothes that you no longer want. Giving back at any stage in our life is possible; you have to look at how you can give back and keep developing the habit of giving back no matter how small you start so that you will be able to give and contribute in a big way when you have more money, resources, and time.

When I first came to the US, I went to a food bank for monthly groceries. Every time I'd go, I saw the people who served me. I became interested in them; I wanted to be like them someday, helping someone in need. However, I was busy with a child with special needs and trying to understand the culture. I was working on getting my life together in the USA. I didn't have the opportunity to serve right away. However, I kept the attitude to serve every time I went to get my groceries.

It wasn't long before I saw a real opportunity to serve; it wasn't much, but I jumped at the chance. I volunteered in my community, interpreting for free at doctor's offices or where needed. My oral English was excellent, and I had a friendly smile that made people feel calm. I volunteered whenever I got the chance. While doing that, I met a dedicated woman who ran a nonprofit organization and served her community. We had a conversation, and she invited me to her office. I was having a challenge looking for work at the time, and I found another opportunity to volunteer. I heard this wonderful woman saying that the city of San Jose organizes an annual "Refugee Day," an event that includes dance/music exhibitions from different ethnic communities. She mentioned that Africans don't participate despite the rich culture. I told her I could organize a dance group since I love dancing. Although my time was very limited, we pulled it off. We demonstrated a dance from East Africa, and I have been doing it every year since. I also saw my opportunity to volunteer as a mentor parent for parents of special need children, after a parent helped me with my son's special needs.

Please don't get me wrong; sometimes, I volunteer more, sometimes less, depending on my schedule and how many things are going on in my life. There was a time when I was going through a hard time with my son being sick all the time; I took a break from volunteering for some time, and then another time when I had my second son until he was one. But I always went back to it. I always kept the attitude of, "How may I serve with what I have now?"

When the time came for me to give in a more significant way, the same attitude led me to start my nonprofit organization to help children with special needs and their parents here in the USA and especially in Eritrea, where I am originally from. I named my nonprofit in honor of my son Aaron. If you are interested in learning more about this nonprofit, visit www.aaronkfoundation.org.

Start where you are. If you currently don't have the time, energy, or money, to give back, start asking how you can serve every day. You will see ways you can contribute to your community. It may be your neighbor, even if it's giving your neighbor a friendly smile and hello, it is enough.

When you find the time or energy, start giving back small, leading you to give back a little more when you find more time. It becomes part of you; one day, you will give back in a way you never thought you could, maybe even to both your country of origin and your new country.

You might also see things you don't like in your community, some things you would like to change, some things you're uncomfortable with that you complain about. Instead of accepting what is, these situations call you forth to be a leader in your community and your surroundings to change the situation.

Maybe you hate that your American neighbors don't interact with one another, so instead of complaining about it and settling into your misery, perhaps you can talk to some of the neighbors around you, host a party, and share your culture. Tell them what being a neighbor means to you and how you would like to know them better. Without knowing it, you have become a leader in your neighborhood who changed the norm, and you'll be surprised that you will find people who will follow your example and keep the party going.

If you hate racism, as most of us do, you can create something that addresses racism in your community. If your kids are bullied at school, you can create or join a group of parents who feel the same as you, so you can be advocates for your children as one voice and create a program that will help kids learn what to do.

The world is not perfect, so don't look for perfection. Instead, be a leader in what is important to you, rather than complaining and being a bitter person. All great leaders are born through adversity; look at the lives of Dr. Martin Luther King Jr., Gandhi, and Nelson Mandela. They didn't just decide that they would be leaders; they didn't like the circumstances around them and had a great desire to change them instead of settling and complaining. They decided to do something about it, and many people who felt the same way followed them, which caused a lot of positive change to their surroundings.

So, when you are ready, become a leader in something you believe in and fight for it. You never know what your potential is until you speak and fight for your truth.

It's been such a pleasure writing this book. It's my way of giving back to the immigrant community because I believe a well-integrated immigrant is a fantastic asset to the US culture, a culture built on immigrants from all over the world.

I hope this book will help you put the pieces together and show you the skills you need at every stage of the integration process—to feel entirely at home here in America. I believe you are unique, brave, and a leader that this country is proud to have. In short, you are home! So enjoy the ride and keep going. See you in my next book.

ACKNOWLEDGMENTS

First and foremost, I would like to thank God for giving me the strength and wisdom to write this book and the source of power in everything that I do.

I want to thank my champion husband for his love and encouragement to be who I want to be to achieve my goals. I want to thank him for being the man I need in my life to do what is important to me. Last but not least, I would like to thank him for his critical thinking and technical support in editing this book.

My boys Aaron, Joseph, and Michael for their joyous presence in my life. For teaching me to be curious and think like a child again. For the challenges they bring to our lives so we can grow with them.

I also would like to thank my mom, Zewdie Shifare Tesfaselassie, and my dad, Mesfin Abraha Mehari, for their courage to leave everything they knew and move to the USA to be a support for Aaron and me. And then for deciding to become American citizens and make their home here. For not being afraid of change, I get courage and bravery from them. I thank them for being my rock and for being amazing grandparents to our three sons, for continually encouraging me and putting up with my absence when I sneaked out to write. This book would not be possible without their sacrifice and generosity.

I want to thank my women's group, WomenKin. Mary Alden Goulart, Catherine Ford, Rebecca Gaspar, Kathy Konjuh, Bonny June. For being there for me, witnessing my cultural integration process, creating the space for me to be undone and becoming a better version of myself. I watched them integrate into the new culture I was bringing to the table as well, and I am incredibly proud to call them my spiritual sisters, whom I tell everything. Their emotional and spiritual support means the world to me, and plays a huge part in my continuous growth.

I want to express my gratitude to all my friends and family for their direct and indirect support.

Thanks to Ms. Clara Adams for teaching me to identify my needs and speak differently to different groups in my life. For believing in me and what I can do and empowering me to be the woman I was striving to become and break free of some of the cultural beliefs I held so firmly that didn't serve me any longer.

I want to thank Theo Cope for creating the space for me to understand who I was, helping me ask important questions that were important for my growth.

A special thank you to Rebecca and Melissa Gaspar for proofreading this book with a tight deadline. I am grateful for your generous heart and your precious time spent on this book.

Acknowledgments

Last but not least, my publisher, Willa Robinson, for her constant encouragement, hard work in shaping my book into what it needs to be. I admire her dedication to publishing this book even when times were tough and challenging.

ABOUT THE AUTHOR

Senait Mesfin Piccagallo is a cultural integration and empowerment coach and author that speaks and writes in three languages: Tigrinya, Amharic, and English. She started writing when she was ten years old, and her family, friends, and colleagues have encouraged her to be an author ever since. Senait kept journals as she navigated transitions from Ethiopia to Eritrea, to China, and then to the US.

In China, she helped teachers prepare English curriculum while working as an English language instructor in Dalian. Senait received a bachelor's degree in sociology and anthropology from Asmara University in East Africa. She resides in northern California with her husband and three children.

She resides in northern California with her husband and three children.

CPSIA information can be obtained
at www.ICGtesting.com
Printed in the USA
LVHW051653020721
691744LV00010B/727